Touch Me Guide to Healing

It's time to heal the church to heal the world

by

Jenny Hagemeyer

iUniverse, Inc.
Bloomington

TOUCH ME GUIDE TO HEALING
IT'S TIME TO HEAL THE CHURCH TO HEAL THE WORLD

Scripture quotations marked NKJ are taken from the New King James Version
Copyright @ 1979, 1980, 1982 by Thomas Nelson, Inc.
Used by permission. All rights reserved

Scripture quotations marked AMP are taken from the AMPLIFIED BIBLE, Old Testament copyright @ 1965 by the Zondervan Corporation. The Amplified New Testament copyright 1958, 1987 by the Lockman Foundation. Used by permission.

Scripture quotations marked NIV are taken from the NEW INTERNATIONAL VERSION. Copyright @ 1973, 1978, 1984 by International Bible Society, Used by permission of Zondervan Publishing House. All rights reserved.

Scripture quotations taken from The Message copyright @ 1993, 1994, 1995, 1996, 2000, 2001, 2002 used by permission of Nav Press Publishing Group.

iUniverse books may be ordered through booksellers or by contacting:

iUniverse
1663 Liberty Drive
Bloomington, IN 47403
www.iuniverse.com
1-800-Authors (1-800-288-4677)

ISBN: 978-1-4620-4669-0 (sc)
ISBN: 978-1-4620-4670-6 (ebk)

Printed in the United States of America

iUniverse rev. date: 10/27/2011

Foreword

I met Jenny years ago when I was a Lieutenant in the County jail and I had a female inmate attempt to commit suicide. Fortunately I was able to stop her in time from hurting herself. It was a Saturday and I couldn't get in touch with the Correctional Facility Counselor. I called the crisis hotline and no one answered. I asked the young lady if there was anyone I could call to talk too. She said she was involved with a woman's group with Jenny Hagemeyer. I then called Jenny, explained the situation to her and put the girl on the phone to talk to her. She was able to help her and then dropped whatever plans she had to come see her that day. That was when I knew she was a special caring person.

I have since gotten to know her better and she is someone truly touched by God who has a message to share about his love and healing power for our spirits. This is revealed not only in her life but also in her book and her ministry. I heartily recommend her book to everyone, especially to those who are hurting inside and long for relief. She will help show you the way and who can provide that peace and sanctuary that you desire. So read it and see for yourself.

Bernie Zook
Warden, Mifflin County Correctional Facility
Lewistown, PA

Introduction

The book *"Touch Me"* was **written** under the inspiration of the Holy Spirit. As I was anxiously waiting to receive my first copy, the Holy Spirit spoke this into my heart. "I am calling you to develop a curriculum on healing."

So, what is a curriculum and what does God want to accomplish?

The definition of curriculum is a regular or particular course of study. (Funk and Wagnall)

There are many nuggets which consist of dreams, visions and God's spoken and written word throughout the book that bring encouragement that God is in control of everything! In order to allow the Holy Spirit to plant these truths into your heart to bring growth to your spirit you will need to study and meditate on His words!

"Taste and see that the LORD is good; blessed is the man who takes refuge in Him." (Psalm 34:8 NIV)

One day I felt my blood sugar dropping since I hadn't eaten anything and it was almost noon. I began to devour a piece of cake and literally wolfed it down. All of a sudden I began to choke until tears began streaming down my face and my throat ached. The Holy Spirit spoke to me at that moment! He said, "I want you to savor your food."

The meaning of savor is to taste or enjoy with pleasure; relish; zest. (Funk and Wagnall)

Afterwards, I began to see that I didn't taste my food even when I sat down at the table at mealtime. I hadn't known this was so difficult for me. My focus was on getting it done and on to the next chore. I wasn't focused on the food and allowing my brain and taste buds to unite to let me know that I was full! I must say that has not been easy for me. Especially when I have so many distractions and my mind wants to wander. I seek God everyday to help me since I have lacked the discipline in this area of my life. Did you notice I thought of mealtime as a chore? A chore is an unpleasant or hard task. (Funk and Wagnall) It certainly wasn't pleasurable and I didn't relish the thought of taking the time out of my busy schedule.

Has it been a chore for you to sit down and savor God's word? Do you have many distractions along with a wandering mind when you come to Jesus table to eat of His choice food?

Jeremiah 17:9 says, "The heart is deceitful above all things, and it is exceedingly perverse and corrupt and severely mortally sick! Who can know it (perceive, understand, be acquainted with his own heart and mind)?" (AMP)

Just as we need our taste buds to unite with our mind, we need God to unite with our mind and heart so He can bring His revelations that will bring His manifestations in our mind, will and emotion.

Are you ready to get real before God, yourself and others? If so please pray this with me before beginning the guide to healing.

Father, your Word says that the heart is deceitful and exceedingly perverse and corrupt. You are the only one that knows my heart. I ask you to look inside of me and reveal the areas in my heart and mind that have kept me from having the freedom that you desire for my life. I ask you to be Lord of every area that needs your healing touch! Thank you that as I study this book and guide, I will taste and see that you are a good God. I confess that I have been in control of my life. I give you complete control and allow you to give me your plan. Thank you for rooting out what needs to be rooted, healing what needs to be healed and restoring what needs to be restored. I receive your blessings since I have taken refuge in you. I look forward with great expectation for you to show yourself strong. In Jesus' Name. Amen.

As you seek the Lord to help you to reflect on Him and savor His word, this guide to healing will enable you to **"Taste and see that the Lord is good!"** He has a great plan for you on your quest to know and love Him!

Now let's get started on your new journey that brings His healing power!

God loves you,

Jenny

Touch Me

Read page 1 in the book *"Touch Me"*.

1.   What is the exciting news?

Are you ready for a change? If not, why?

Do you believe God wants to spend time with you? Why or why not?

Who are you? Read and meditate on the following scriptures.

The Hebrew word for **meditate** is *siyach* which means to declare, speak, and converse with oneself aloud.

- You are God's child .... I John 3:2

- You are a new creature.......................... II Corinthians 5:17

- You are created in His image .... Genesis 1:27

- You are from God .... I John 4:4

- You are His workmanship .... Ephesians 2:10

- You are the apple of His eye .... Psalm 17:8

- You are alive to God............................. Romans 6:11

- You are loved by God........................... I Thessalonians 1:4

- You have the mind of Christ .... I Corinthians 2:16

Let's take a look at I Corinthians 2:14-16.

But the natural, non spiritual man does not accept or welcome or admit into his heart the gifts and teachings and revelations of the Spirit of God, for they are folly (meaningless nonsense) to him; and he is incapable of knowing them (of progressively recognizing, understanding, and becoming better acquainted with them) because they are spiritually discerned and estimated and appreciated.

But the spiritual man tries all things (he examines, investigates, inquires into, questions, and discerns all things), yet is himself to be put on trial and judged by no one (he can read the meaning of everything, but no one can properly discern or appraise or get an insight into him). For who has known or understood the mind (the counsels and purposes) of the Lord so as to guide and instruct Him and give Him knowledge? But we have the mind of Christ (the Messiah) and do hold the thoughts (feelings and purposes) of His heart. (AMP)

2.   What does this scripture hold for you?

Now speak these scriptures out loud over yourself:

- I **am** a child of God

- I **am** a new creature

- I **am** created in His image

- I **am** from God and greater is He in me than he that is in the world

- I **am** His workmanship created by God to do His good works

- I **am** the apple of God's eye

- I **am** dead to sin and alive to God through Christ Jesus

- I **am** loved by God

- I **have** the mind of Christ

Read page 2 and refer to the image in the book *"Touch Me"*.

Has God been speaking to you that it's time to step out?

Is fear of making the wrong moves for God (is this God or me) or fear of what you will look like to others holding you back?

Job 42:2 says, "I know that you can do all things; no plan of yours can be thwarted."(NIV)

Do you really believe that? If not, why?

God gave me a revelation that no matter what happens in my life nothing can succeed against the Lord. Have you received that same revelation from the Lord? If not, whether you are alone in this study or in a group take this time and ask God for His divine revelation that will change your heart and mind.

Read pages 3-4 in the book *"Touch Me"*.

Most of us have problems with changes in our lives. Even though we are not happy about our circumstances we aren't comfortable with changes in our life. We become use to the same old same olds and don't like when God begins to take us out of our comfort zones.

My husband and I had caught a bunny escapee from a neighbor's cage. Since our neighbors decided they didn't want him back, my husband built a fence around him and put a small crate for the bunny to have shelter. The following week he decided to build him a larger home with a ramp. My husband and I were so excited to see how he would react. On his first visit to his home he slid down the ramp. He was so upset that he went back to his little crate. For the rest of that week he didn't go near his new home and continued to be cramped in his little crate. One day I decided to have Fred take his crate away that would hopefully encourage him to seek for shelter in his new home.

Well, the bunny got so upset that he ran around in circles looking for his little crate.

When God is trying to give you His best have you felt like the little bunny looking for your comfort zone? If so, what did you do?

My husband was blessing the bunny with the best shelter yet the bunny was not looking at it with Fred's perspective.

Are you looking at your situations through God's eyes or your own perspective?

3.   What do the following scriptures all have in common: Hebrews 12:2, Isaiah 46:8-10 and Revelations 21:6? (NIV)

Read page 5 in the book *"Touch Me"*.

The definition of adversity is a condition of hardship or affliction. (Funk and Wagnall)

4.   Satan has a goal and God has a purpose in adversity. What is it?

Are you recognizing satan's goal and reaching for God's purpose or allowing satan's goal to keep you from reaching for God's purpose?

5.   Read and meditate on Romans 12:2 (NKJ) on page 5 in the book *"Touch Me"*. Why is it important to renew your mind with the word of God?

6.   When your mind is being renewed with the word of God what takes place in your soul and spirit?

Refer to the image on page 5 in the book *"Touch Me"*.

7.   How do we place Jesus on part of the cross?

Read pages 6-7 in the book *"Touch Me"*.

8.   How does an eruption of a volcano compare with the Holy Spirit within us?

9.   What is the acronym given for each letter of the word abundant?

Are you living an abundant life or is your life full of discouragement?

Do you see yourself as a victim of your past and surrounding circumstances or are you aware of the victory in laying down all of your burdens for God to have the opportunity to show Himself strong?

Do you really want to change? If so, are you ready for an encounter with God?

Bold

Read and meditate on Hebrews 4:15-16 on page 8 in the book ***"Touch Me"***.

We need to come boldly to the throne of grace. What does that mean to you?

Refer to the image on page 8 in the book ***"Touch Me"***.

Are you coming to the Lord with frankness (no beating around the bush), forthrightness (moving right in and getting to the point), and outspokenness (speaking your mind), or do you tiptoe through the tulips and speak spiritual jargon to the Lord?

Read pages 9-10 in the book ***"Touch Me"***.

Read and meditate on Luke 8:27-40.

1.   How was the crowd waiting for Jesus?

How have you been waiting for Jesus to answer you?

2.   When the man was delivered from the legion of demons that had tormented him for years what did Jesus commission him to do?

Jesus freed this man from the pain and torment of his past and from the bondage of so many years. Satan thought this man was dead spiritually, physically and emotionally.

Do you have a defining moment to share or do you feel that you have been pronounced dead by the enemy and don't feel or see the light of Jesus in your life?

Most of our spiritual bondage is not easily detected like the man with the legion of demons. However, if we don't ask the Lord to show us what is in our hearts we will reject the process of healing in our heart and mind.

If you have prayed the prayer in the introduction, expect Jesus to reveal those areas in your heart that have held you in bondage. As He reveals those areas of pride, unforgiveness, selfishness, jealousy, bitterness, resentment, fear, and worry give these areas of your heart to him and allow him to shine His light into the darkness of your heart and mind daily.

When we have a need of healing physically, emotionally and spiritually we have many thoughts running through our minds. I believe there were many thoughts in this crowd of people waiting for Jesus. (Review pages 10-11 in the book *"Touch Me"*.) Maybe some were very negative and fearful and some were very hopeful.

When you have waited for Jesus to heal you . . . . what thoughts have you experienced in your mind?

Read and meditate on Luke 8:41 on page 11 in the book *"Touch Me"*.

Jairus was a religious leader of the synagogue. Some of the religious leaders mocked Jesus even though they watched many of His miracles. Notice Jairus didn't tap Jesus on the shoulder or ask Jesus to come. He fell at Jesus feet with brokenness for his twelve year old daughter whom he loved very much.

When is the last time you fell at Jesus' feet and wept for your loved one's salvation or healing?

Let's take a look at Psalm 51:17 on page 11 in the book *"Touch Me"*.

The definition of contrite is to be deeply and humbly remorseful for one's sins. (Funk and Wagnall)

Jairus came to Jesus with brokenness in his spirit and heart that caused Jesus to stop and receive his sacrifice. Perhaps Jairus would never have come to Jesus if he hadn't been driven by his grief.

Do you know anyone who came to Jesus through grief after many years of rejecting Him?

When was the last time you came before God with a broken spirit and a broken and deeply humbled remorseful heart for your sins and for others?

Take this time to ask the Lord to give you brokenness for the things that break his heart in you and others.

Read and meditate on Luke 8:43-44.

A woman who had suffered from a flow of blood for twelve years and was beyond the medical capabilities suddenly was touching the hem of Jesus' garment.

3.   Wasn't Jesus going to Jairus' house? Why did she receive her healing before Jairus' daughter? After all, he came to Jesus first.

I believe that God always answers our prayers with yes, no or wait!

Have you ever been praying and believing for another person's prayers to be answered only to find God answered the other person's and you are still waiting? How did you react?

4.   Now this woman not only touched Jesus but received her healing immediately. So . . . . why is she afraid to admit that she touched Him?

5.   Review and list the possible ten questions in her mind on pages 12-13 in the book *"Touch Me"*.

6.   What does she have to do before she can step forward?

7.   In Luke 8:47-48 the woman falls at Jesus feet trembling and tells Him why she touched him. What was Jesus response?

Read the revelation of being God's daughter on pages 13-15 in the book *"Touch Me"*.

8.   What is the Hebrew word **Bath** mean? Have you received a revelation that you are the apple of His eye? If not, Sons and Daughters, pray this with me.

Father, help me to see that I am the apple of your eye. I ask you to give me a revelation of who I am and who you are to me. I shut the door to the enemy's negative words in my mind and open my heart and mind to hear your words. In Jesus' Name. Amen.

Read and meditate on Luke 8:49-50.

9.   It looked like all hope was gone. Jairus' beloved daughter had died. It was beyond the midnight hour for a miracle. What possible thoughts did Jairus have? Read page15 in the book **"Touch Me"**.

Read page 16 in the book **"Touch Me"**.

In Luke 8:50 Jesus is saying, "Don't be afraid only believe and she will be made well."

Let's look at two words . . . . **only believe**! Perhaps it looks like all hope is gone in your life and nothing is ever going to change. If you are in a group setting reach out and take each other's hand. If you are studying this alone reach out and imagine God holding your hand. Pray this with me.

Jesus, I ask you to help my unbelief. I give you this fear and connect my faith with yours to believe for . . . . (be specific). Forgive me for believing satan's words over your WORD!! Thank you for showing yourself strong in this situation. In Jesus' Name. Amen.

Read pages 16-22 for my testimony in the book **"Touch Me"**.

For many years I only knew God as a Bible God. Do you see God as a Bible God or is He your personal Savior? In other words, have you grown up in church knowing about Him or do you know and hear from him daily?

If you have never heard him speaking to you do you believe that God wants to talk with you every day? If not, why?

I believe that God talks to us every day but there are many reasons that block us from hearing his voice.

When your house is cluttered with a lot of objects it creates confusion and chaos in your home. When your mind is cluttered with all kinds of negative thoughts it too creates chaos and confusion, therefore enabling you to listen to the negative thoughts which contradict God's word for your situations.

1 Corinthians 14:33 (NKJ) says, "For God is not the author of confusion, but of peace, as in all churches of the saints."

So, is your spiritual house in order or is it in a disarray of denial, contradiction and resistance to God's spoken and written word?

John 7:38 (AMP) says, "He who believes in Me (who cleaves to and trusts in and relies on me) as the Scripture has said, from his innermost being shall flow (continuously) springs and rivers of living water."

Are you cleaving, trusting and relying on God and receiving His living water like a sponge into your spirit or is your spirit dry, parched and in need of His living water?

Have you or anyone else close to you experienced a divorce? If so, what part of my testimony can you identify with?

Read the story of the little boy who picked up stones on page 22 in the book ***"Touch Me"***.

Have you been picking up burdens that are too heavy for you?

Take this time and boldly name your burdens. If you are in a group setting divide into groups of two and pray for each other. One person confesses a burden such as worry or fear and gives it to Jesus verbally. The other person prays for her or him.

Undefeated

Do you see yourself as defeated by the enemy or undefeated because of Jesus death and resurrection?

Read pages 23-24 in the book *"Touch Me"*.

The first part of John 10:10 says, **"The thief comes only in order to steal, kill and destroy."**

- The Greek meaning of steal is filch. (Strong's)

- The definition of filch is to steal slyly and in small amounts. (Funk and Wagnall)

- The Greek meaning of kill is immolate or slaughter for any purpose. (Strong's)

- The definition of immolate is to kill as a sacrificial victim. (Funk and Wagnall)

- The Greek meaning of destroy is perish. (Strong's)

- The definition of perish is to suffer a violent or untimely death. (Funk and Wagnall)

As I was studying and meditating on this verse I thought of a fox and how it sneaks up slowly, little by little, patiently waiting for the right moment to kill (immolate) its victim. A fox is nocturnal which means that he sees very well in the dark and usually attacks when the lambs are sleeping or have wandered away from the shepherd. Suddenly without warning the fox seizes his opportunity to attack and the baby lambs perish.

Notice . . . . the fox usually attacks when the lambs are sleeping or have wandered away from the shepherd.

There is a story about a sheep farmer, Ian Whalen, in Australia who was losing many of his lambs to the predator foxes. One night in his frustration a thought occurred to him. Shepherds often slept with the sheep to protect them. He realized that he needed to invent something that would take the place of his presence since the winters are too harsh for him to sleep outside. He created an invention called the "Fox lights." Foxes don't have a problem with regular flashing lights since they are able to get used to seeing them in the dark. However, an irregular light is much harder for them to accept and produces a threat of a presence in the paddock (a field in the agricultural sense). With this invention he found that sheep are just the opposite. They are not afraid and actually draw closer to the lights.

The light was invented to keep the predator fox out of the agricultural field and draw the sheep and lambs closer to the light that would remove any fear of their predators and guide their feet on the right path.

I am reminded of the following scripture in Luke 1:79 (AMP) which says, "To shine upon and give light to those who sit in darkness and in the shadow of death, to direct and guide our feet in a straight line into the way of peace."

Jesus came to shine His light on the darkness of our life. Without that light of His presence we live in darkness and the shadow of death is encompassed in our soul.

Because if you acknowledge and confess with your lips that Jesus is Lord and in your heart believe (adhere to, trust in, and rely on the truth) that God raised Him from the dead, you will be saved. (Romans 10:9 AMP)

If we (freely) admit that we have sinned and confess our sins, He is faithful and just (true to His own nature and promises) and will forgive our sins (dismiss our lawlessness) and (continuously) cleanse us from all

unrighteousness (everything not in conformity to His will in purpose, thought, and action). (I John 1:9 AMP)

Maybe you haven't asked Jesus into your heart because you felt the darkness of the sin was too great for God to forgive. Or maybe you haven't accepted Him into your heart because you have thought you have plenty of time. None of us know the day or the hour when death will come knocking at our door. Are you ready? If not, today is your day to make Jesus the Lord of your life! Pray this with me.

Jesus, I confess that I am a sinner and I ask you to forgive me. I believe that you died for my sins and have been raised from the dead so I can live as you have planned for my life. I ask you to come into my heart and cleanse me from all unrighteousness and I now make you the Lord of my life! In Jesus' Name. Amen

Congratulations! You have joined the family of God and now have the light of His presence to direct your path.

When we confess our sins, He is faithful and just to forgive our sins and to cleanse us from all unrighteousness. We now have His light to guide and direct our footsteps away from the enemy of our soul and receive His peace. As the fox is threatened by the presence of this light, the evil predator (satan) is also threatened by the presence of God's great light. Without the presence of God in our lives we remain prey to the devil's schemes and are helpless and without hope! With the light of God's presence we become more aware of the devil patiently and slyly stalking us little by little. When we continue to see the light of God's love we place all of our hope in Him! Now we no longer remain in hopeless despair that causes us to perish.

So, how do we resist the devil's schemes?

Read and meditate on Song of Solomon 2:15 (AMP).

My heart was touched and I fervently sang to him my desire. Take for us the foxes, the little foxes that spoil the vineyards (of our love), for our vineyards are in blossom.

Fervently means moved by or showing great warmth or intensity as of emotion or enthusiasm; ardent; very hot and burning. (Funk and Wagnall)

Little foxes were coming into the vineyard gnawing on the roots little by little which eventually would destroy the blossoms and keep the vines from producing fruit.

So . . . . what little foxes have been coming into your life hindering your relationship with God and holding you back from receiving His fruit of the Spirit?

Write them down on a piece of paper. If you are in a group place all the papers in the middle on a table and pray this prayer with me.

Jesus, I give every area of my life that is hindering me from my relationship you with you and holding me back from receiving your fruit of the Spirit in my life. Forgive me for placing my focus on the things of this earth and not on you. I desire a hot and burning love for you that will change my heart and help me to choose your plan for my life.

When your heart is hot and burning for God you can make the decision to not allow the enemy to spoil the vineyard of your love for Him and to choose to allow God to produce the fruit of His spirit within you!

David had a burning love for God and didn't allow Goliath's taunting jeers to inject poisonous darts of fear to steal His fruit of peace.

Refer to the first image on page 24 in the book, *"Touch Me"*.

1. I was in a situation where fear was maintaining a hold on my emotions. List and discuss fourteen encouraging statements spoken by the Lord when I cried out to him.

2. Because I was afraid of being hurt, what was the fear blocking me from receiving?

Refer to image at the bottom of page 24-25 in the book, *"Touch Me"*.

3.   What was God's desire in giving me this vision?

Psalm 112:8 says, "His heart is secure, he will have no fear. In the end he will look in triumph on his foes."

When a situation comes up that could place you in fear, do you see yourself confident in the arms of Jesus or trapped in a burning building of fear?

I Samuel 17:24 says, "And all the men in Israel, when they saw the man, fled from him and were dreadfully afraid." (NKJ)

4.   Why were the Israelites full of fear?

5.   What probably prevented the Philistines from a full quick attack?

Have you ever been paralyzed with fear? Where was your focus?

Refer to the first image on page 26 in the book, *"Touch Me"*.

6.   Who was the Israelite's greatest enemy, the Red Sea or the Egyptians?

7.   When God began to root fear out of me, what did He speak into my heart?

Refer to image on bottom of page 26 in the book, *"Touch Me"*.

This drama was portrayed as God's plan and satan's plot. Are you proving God's word or believing satan's lies?

Read page 27 in the book *"Touch Me"*.

For forty days and nights the Israelites heard Goliath's taunting jeers. They not only saw the giant that brought so much fear but they believed his words over God's word! Because they were focused on the fear they could not receive the love that God had for them. God needed someone that he could show himself strong through.

Read and meditate on the scripture I Samuel 17:20 in the book **"Touch Me".**

Rose is taken from a Hebrew word that means to incline. (Strong's)

David spent time with the Lord and inclined his heart to hear from the Lord daily.

Read and meditate on Joshua 24:23 in the book **"Touch Me".**

8.   Joshua gave the Israelites two commands. What were they?

The foreign gods represented idols of wood, stone and gold. They could not serve God with all their hearts as long as these idols were in their lives. When our desires are divided with pleasure, fame, money and hidden sins that remain in the closets of our hearts, God will not be able to occupy the highest place in our heart and have full control of our lives. Take this time and allow the Holy Spirit to examine your heart for any idols that have occupied part of your heart and pray this with me.

Holy Spirit, I ask you to examine my heart and show me where my heart has been divided by idols in my life that I am not aware of and reveal these idols to me. Those idols that I am aware of I give to you . . . (name them if you are by yourself) and ask you to forgive me for making them the desires of my heart. I give you the highest place in my heart and full control over my life. In Jesus' Name. Amen.

David did not allow the enemy to steal, kill or destroy his mind with fear. He knew who his Champion was and placed his focus on Him! God had been with him when a lion and bear tried to kill the sheep and now he knew that God would never leave or forsake him.

Notice . . . . David did not allow the enemy to steal. Whatever situation you are in right now . . . . are you allowing God to permeate your heart and mind with His word or giving territory to the enemy and listening to his words of defeat?

Take this time and reflect on your past. How has God showed you how He has been with you in the midst of your trial? Where was your focus?

Refer to image on page 27 in the book, ***"Touch Me"***.

The Lord showed me that our spirit is to be as strong as the "Hulk!" We cannot fight our battles in the flesh but must fight them in the spirit!

Read and meditate on I Samuel 17:14-26.

David came out to greet his brothers. In verse 23 all the men, including David, saw and heard Goliath's threats. Let's compare David's response with that of the Israelites.

The Israelite's fled the scene. They were hiding like cowards and allowing the enemy to keep them in the bondage of fear! In verse 23 they were listening to satan's taunting words through Goliath instead of listening to their God.

Whenever a fearful situation comes into my life I am learning to say "I am not moved by what I see or hear but I am moved by what I know!" Fear contradicts the word of FAITH!

David saw Goliath and heard the same words as the Israelite army. However, he was not moved by what he saw but was moved by what he knew! He knew his undefeated Champion God! He was not in the army of men but in the army of the Lord!

David's comment in verse 26 was "What shall be done for the man who kills this Philistine and takes away the reproach from Israel? For who is this uncircumcised Philistine that he should defy the armies of the living God?"

Notice he didn't say, **"If** he kills him." He made a **declaration of faith** that it would happen.

Can you picture David's spirit rising up? David didn't look at the man. He looked at the Creator of the man.

The Israelite's saw Goliath's defiance of Israel. David saw the defiance against the armies of his God. How dare he come up against our God!

On page 28 in the book *"Touch Me"* David was aware of three things:

- The attack was from the enemy;

- He knew the nature of the enemy;

- He exercised his authority over the enemy.

Okay, let's take a look at these three things:

This was a full frontal attack! The enemy wasn't keeping anything hidden from them. He had shown himself full force and was ready to destroy the army of the Lord. David knew the nature of the enemy and how he kept the Israelites in the bondage of fear. David knew that he couldn't listen to the enemy's words so he spoke words of faith that counteracted the fear.

While I was working on this study I talked with a lady who was hit with a full frontal attack on her health. It all began with a vision that was demonic which brought confusion and fear. Even though she asked the Lord to protect her she received a sudden health problem. As I was praying for her and seeking the Lord for His word . . . . I heard the Lord say, "This is a full frontal attack!" When the enemy showed himself through this vision immediately it should have been *rejected*. Instead she received a spirit of expectation that something was going to happen. The Lord showed me that we needed to exercise His authority over the enemy by taking authority over the spirit of fear and confusion in Jesus' Name. She no longer accepted the enemy's plot for her life but rejected it. Then we applied God's word to her situation and spoke healing over her body. As other prayer warriors prayed and anointed her, she began to heal daily and the physical pain began to leave.

In (this) freedom Christ has made us free (and completely liberated us); stand fast then, and do not be hampered and held ensnared and submit again to a yoke of slavery (which you have once put off).
(Galatians 5:1 AMP)

What attacks are you expecting from the enemy instead of rejecting them?

If you are in a group setting, share them with each other. Afterwards, pray this with me:

Jesus, thank you for dying on the cross so that I could be made free and completely liberated. I reject fear etc. (name whatever the enemy is trying or has placed on you) in Jesus Name and reject any expectations of what the enemy wants to do. I now stand fast and will not be hampered or ensnared by any bondage the enemy wants to place me in. I look forward with great expectation for you to show yourself strong in my heart and mind. In Jesus' Name. Amen.

When you have a negative expectation that something is going to happen you give satan the opportunity to produce a negative result in your life.

When you have a positive expectation that something is going to happen your faith gives God the opportunity to produce a positive result.

Read page 29 in the book *"Touch Me"*.

David resisted the devil and he fled. However, now satan tries to come through a family member.

Now Eliab his eldest brother heard what he said to the men; and Eliab's anger was kindled against David and he said, "Why did you come here? With whom have you left those few sheep in the wilderness? I know your presumption and evilness of heart; for you came down that you might see the battle." (I Samuel 17:28 AMP)

Why was Eliab spewing those angry hurtful words to his brother? Perhaps David's brother was jealous. After all, how would it look to the other Israelites if Eliab was full of fear and his baby brother spoke words of faith?

More importantly! Let's look at how Eliab felt about himself. Notice Eliab completely changed the subject and directed his anger at David. He tried to put him down by speaking words of condemnation to make himself look better. Satan through Eliab was conducting an inspection of David's ulterior motives so Eliab wouldn't look at the fear that was in his own heart. As long as he didn't face the fear it remained in the darkness of his heart!

Let's take a look at where the jealousy may have ignited towards his baby brother or where it may have begun.

Read and meditate on I Samuel 16:1-13.

God had spoken to Samuel that He had rejected Saul as King and was sending him to anoint one of Jesse's sons. God gave Samuel a plan of inviting Jesse and his sons to consecrate themselves and attend a sacrifice to the Lord. Samuel initiated an inspection of all Jesse's sons beginning with Eliab the eldest of the siblings. Samuel's first impression of Eliab's appearance and stature was, "this must be the man." After all Eliab's name meant "My God is Father." However, God told Samuel that man looks at the outward appearance but God looks at the heart.

God through Samuel rejected Eliab and his other siblings but chose their baby brother David in front of them all.

Read and meditate on the following scriptures.

But now your kingdom shall not continue; the Lord has sought out (David) a man after His own heart, and the Lord has commanded him to be prince and ruler over His people, because you have not kept what the Lord commanded you. (I Samuel 13:14)

And he disposed him. He raised up David to be their king; of him He bore witness and said, "I have found David son of Jesse a man after My own heart, who will do all My will and carry out My program." (Acts 13:22 AMP)

9.   What did God look for in anointing a King?

10.   What did God see in David's heart?

God saw the wickedness in Saul's heart and dethroned him. Perhaps that is why he did not choose Eliab. So what was in Eliab's heart for God to reject him? Perhaps jealousy had been in his heart from childhood. Saul had the darkness of jealousy in his heart and did not have a willing spirit to carry out God's plan for the children of Israel. Perhaps God saw the same darkness and unwillingness in Eliab's heart.

Can you imagine your baby brother or sister receiving an anointing from God for the position that you should have? How would you feel?

Have you ever been in sibling rivalry? How did you feel about yourself? C'mon be honest!

Perhaps God is revealing the darkness of jealousy in your heart towards a sibling or someone else. If so, pray this prayer with me.

Lord, I am sorry for the way I have treated my brother, sister or (other person). Please forgive me. I give you this jealousy that I have carried in my heart for many years that blocks me from receiving your love and blinds me from seeing them through your eyes. Thank you for convicting me of this sin in my heart and bringing restoration to our relationship. I look forward with great expectation for you to show yourself strong in both of our lives. In Jesus' Name. Amen.

Read I Samuel 17:29-30.

Verse 29 constitutes David's first response of defending his innocence.

When someone accuses you unfairly what is your first response?

Verse 30 shows David's focus on what God was calling him to do. He turned and no longer listened to the voice of the enemy through his brother but set his mind and heart on what God's plan was.

While I was working on this study our family encountered some problems that looked impossible to solve. My mind was continually wandering into the negativity which caused my emotions to shift gears into discouragement, worry and fear. I kept seeking the Lord and crying out for His peace. One morning I was sitting under our tree in silence waiting for God to speak to me. A flock of different kinds of birds suddenly were making all sorts of noise. Notice I did not say the birds were singing. Oddly enough I heard some sounds from those birds that I had never heard before. Normally I loved to sit and listen to a beautiful chorus of birds but none of them were in tune. I began to get irritated at these sounds and felt like I wanted to flee the scene. It was at that moment that God began to show me the state of my mind. I was listening to a multitude of negative voices that prevented me from hearing the still small voice of my God! He showed me through those birds that as long as I listened to the voices of negativity I could not hear God's heart for our family. When I walked away in my mind from all the negative comments I began to hear powerful words from God that began to transform my thinking! With my focus back on God's word for our family I now could see God's perspective and follow His voice and no longer be led astray by the negative voices. As long as I allowed the enemy to consume my mind he was winning. As soon as I turned my back on the evil I saw the victory in God!

When David turned his back on the enemy who was using his brother's weakness to attack David's weaknesses he saw the victory in God!

Read page 30 in the book ***"Touch Me"***.

David turned what could have been a major disappointment into God's appointment. God was sending David on a mission and had given him a statement of faith. Perhaps you have a disappointment in your life right now.

Is your focus on the disappointment or on God's appointment for your life?

Let's take a look at 1 Samuel 17:44-47 (Amp) which shows David's statement of faith in His God.

The Philistine said to David, "Come to me, and I will give your flesh to the birds of the air and the beasts of the field." Then said David to the Philistine, "You come to me with a sword, a spear, and a javelin, but I come to you in the name of the Lord of hosts, the God of the ranks of Israel, Whom you have defied. This day the Lord will deliver you into my hand, and I will smite you and cut off your head. And I will give the corpses of the army of the Philistines this day to the birds of the air and the wild beasts of the earth, that all the earth may know that there is a

God in Israel. And all this assembly shall know that the Lord saves not with sword and spear; for the battle is the Lord's, and He will give you into our hands."

What is your statement of faith in the midst of a battle?

Do you believe what others or God says about you?

One weekend I had been traveling with a special group of church women that blessed me with an invitation to join them. One of those days we all decided to shop at some outlets with all of us milling around in different stores. While I was shopping I saw a blouse that I thought was really pretty on the hanger but didn't know how it would look on me. There were about three women in the store when I decided to try on the blouse. After I tried the blouse on I looked for someone's opinion. However, all of the women had gone and I was alone to make my own decision. I was disappointed that I didn't have anyone to give me their opinion. However, I decided reluctantly to buy the blouse anyhow.

In the evening we attended a women's seminar. The speaker gave us time to hear from the Holy Spirit before she prayed. Suddenly I felt God's presence and heard him say, "I am freeing you from people's opinions tonight!" God had been telling me to speak to some women at the seminar about my book but my thoughts were what would they think? I wept almost uncontrollably since I hadn't realized that I needed liberated from people's opinions. Afterwards I obeyed God and felt His boldness and courage as I talked with those women. Praise God! He broke those chains that were confining me from moving forward and He set me free!

Perhaps before reading my testimony you hadn't realized that you had a need for people's opinions and now you are saying, "Jenny that's me too!"

If you are not sure ask the Lord to search your heart and reveal the need for people's opinions. If you have realized the need . . . . ask the Holy Spirit to break those chains that have been confining and restricting you from moving forward. Now thank God for His liberation from people's opinions.

Refer to the image on page 30 in the book *"Touch Me"*.

Do you believe that God has already walked ahead of everything that we will experience in this journey?

Read Isaiah 52:12 on page 30 in the book *"Touch Me".*

One day I was sitting outside basking in the sun with the SON! Suddenly I felt the presence of the Lord encompass me behind . . . . before . . . and around me.

Psalm 34:7 says, "The Angel of the Lord encamps around those who fear Him (who revere and worship Him with awe) and each of them He delivers."(AMP)

Think of that! Do you need Him to encompass you with his presence today? He has walked before you and has a plan to work out your problems. He is your rear guard to protect you and is encamped around you. Imagine being in a country all by yourself surrounded by the enemy. Your heart is pounding with fear and you keep running to find new hiding places. Suddenly the military moves in and sets up a camp. You are no longer alone and the fear begins to dissipate. You stop finding places to hide since you have found safety in the military camp.

Think of this! You are in God's military camp. He is the commander-in-chief and has promised to never leave or forsake you.

He says, "Fear not! I am here to defend your cause and set you free. My mighty forces outnumber the enemy." The good news is that God has surrounded you with His presence even when you don't feel Him!

Jeremiah 23:23 says, "Am I a God at hand, says the Lord, and not a God afar off?" (AMP)

Now David is summoned by Saul who has heard the news.

Read and meditate on I Samuel 17:32-37.

In verse 33 Saul looks at David's outward appearance and says that he is not able to fight against the Philistine. However, in verse 37 Saul sends David out with his blessing.

11. What changed Saul's mind?

Refer to page 31 in the book *"Touch Me"*.

Do you believe God has called you to a mission even though you are facing opposition?

When God called me to launch Promise Land Ministries I faced a lot of opposition. I kept seeking God for His wisdom and direction. I knew that I represented the Lord and that it was important how I treated others who opposed me.

One day God spoke this to me. "You don't have to defend what I have given to you. Let me be your defense and I will move mightily on your behalf." Actually, the spirit of opposition helped to develop my character in such a way that a spirit of agreement would not have accomplished! As I chose to forgive others for their insensitivity and obeyed the Lord I watched Him move not only on my behalf but also on behalf of others.

What God has called you to . . . He will keep you! God showed me as I spoke with authority over the circumstance and placed my confidence in Him . . . He was keeping me in the hollow of his hand.

Refer to the image on page 33 in the book *"Touch Me"*.

David didn't hide from the Philistine Goliath. Instead he made God his hiding place.

Are you hiding within yourself or making Him your hiding place?

Are you using your past as an excuse to remain a victim of satan or allowing God to make your past His opportunity to propel you to victory and the plan He has for your life?

Jenny Hagemeyer

I was watching a commercial on television. A little boy was hiding in a tree and thought no one would be able to find him. However, he looked down and was surprised to see his mother. He said, "Mom, how did you find me?" She said, "I would find you wherever you go." The little boy said, "Why?" The mother looked lovingly at her little boy and said, "Because you are a part of me."

That's the love your Father has for you. He knows all of your weaknesses, mistakes and failures and He wants you to give them all to Him. You can run but you can't hide from Him.

You have searched me, Lord, and you know me. You know when I sit and when I rise; you perceive my thoughts from afar. You discern my going out and my lying down; you are familiar with all my ways. Before a word is on my tongue you, Lord, know it completely. You hem me in behind and before, and you lay your hand upon me. Such knowledge is too wonderful for me, too lofty for me to attain. Where can I go from your Spirit? Where can I flee from your presence? (Psalm 139:1-7 NIV)

For you created my inmost being; you knit me together in my mother's womb. I praise you because I am fearfully and wonderfully made; your works are wonderful, I know that full well. My frame was not hidden from you when I was made in the secret place, when I was woven together in the depths of the earth. Your eyes saw my unformed body; all the days ordained for me were written in your book before one of them came to be. (Psalm 139:13-16 NIV)

If you are hiding your weaknesses within yourself and using your past as an excuse to remain a victim of satan . . . . pray this with me.

Lord . . . . Forgive me for using my past as an excuse to remain a victim. I have been hiding my weaknesses within so I would not have to face the pain of my past. I ask you to reveal the darkness that has remained in the closet of my heart for many years. Thank you for making my past your opportunity to propel me to victory and the plan you have for my life. You are my hiding place and my shield. I place my hope in your word. Thank you for being my undefeated Champion!

New

Read pages 34-35 in the book *"Touch Me"* about the woman in mirror.

1. When this woman looks into the mirror what does she see?

2. Where is her focus?

3. Why is the enemy bombarding her mind with discouragement?

4. How does she see herself?

5. What does she need to do in order for God to get rid of the garbage in her life?

6. Why is she allowing the unforgiveness in her heart?

7. Why does she live daily with anxiousness and fear of her future?

8. What keeps her living a mundane life?

9. What keeps her from fulfilling God's plan and purpose for her life?

10. Why doesn't she see the gifts within herself?

When my focus was on myself I could only see my insecurities through a mirror of negativity. When my focus was placed on God I began to look into the mirror of God's word and allow Him to transform me into His image!

Perhaps you can identify with one or more of the questions above. Circle the ones you identify with. If you are in a group discuss them. If you are by yourself talk to the Lord about them.

Which mirror are you looking into?

II Corinthians 3:18 says, "And all of us, as with unveiled face, (because we) continued to behold (in being the Word of God) as in a mirror the glory of the Lord, are constantly transfigured into His very own image in ever increasing splendor and from one degree of glory to another; (for this comes) from the Lord (Who is) the Spirit." (AMP)

God wants to transform you from the inside and give you a new look! He wants to cancel the assignment of low self esteem from the enemy and enable you to be more than a conqueror to gain a surpassing victory through Him.

One day during a tough situation in my life I was driving past a farm. I noticed a little girl skipping down the driveway. God showed me this is what He wanted to accomplish in my heart and mind. As I looked at her she didn't seem to have a care in the world. She was secure in who she was and wasn't afraid of falling as she bounced on one foot at a time. The sunlight bounced off her hair as she played and giggled with great delight.

I realized that was the plan God had for me. I was His little girl and He wanted me to be like this little care free child. But . . . how could I accomplish this on my own? I was feeling anything but carefree. Perhaps as you are reading this you are saying, "I feel like this too." Let me encourage you that God has the best plan for your life. So . . . . let's look at where we begin!

I am convinced that we will never receive our healing without an intimate personal relationship with the Lord! When I knew God as a Bible God and not a personal God I didn't realize the healing that was needed in my heart. Just as your children are an expression of your heart . . . . you are an expression of God's heart! When you begin to see the importance of your birth through God's eyes you will stop looking for your identity through your jobs, marriages and families.

As you sit in the Lord's presence and experience His love . . . . He will become the center of your attention and you will no longer look at yourself, other people or things as important.

When you submit to a God who is not just a God of love . . . . **He is love** . . . . you will realize more of His presence that will bring healing in your heart and mind.

One day the Holy Spirit spoke this in my heart as I felt His love envelop me. "Focus on my love for you. I have a perfect love that dissipates all your burdens. When you focus on my love, your circumstances do not take hold of you. When you focus on my love, you give up all the earthly love that you so desire. I am the only one who can satisfy your soul. When you focus on my love you are not disappointed in others' love for you. They cannot give you what your deep, deep longing inside of you needs. I alone am the one who meets all your needs."

God wants to hear your heart. In the beginning of learning how to spend time in the Lord's presence I started communicating with God by writing letters to Him! I didn't know how to express my heart to Him with spoken words but could bring more expression in writing to Him. I began to talk to Him about everything good and bad, and asked Him to help me become more like Him! As I struggled to convey my feelings during this process my emotions began to manifest.

As I wrote letters to God daily for months I began to hear his heart for my situation. I wasn't writing letters to Him in vain. He was not only reading them but writing His letters on my heart. As I read His letters of love I began to feel His presence in ways I'd never known before and least expected.

I began to trust God with everything in my life. I came to God as a little child telling Him where it hurt.

Mark 10:15 says, "Truly I tell you, whoever does not receive and accept and welcome the kingdom of God like a little child (does) positively shall not enter it at all." (AMP)

I found myself waking up in the morning eager to spend time with my Daddy who was giving me encouragement in the midst of discouragement.

One day as I was going through the divorce of my first marriage I was weeping uncontrollably. I told God how I was rejected. I felt Him sit beside me and cry with me. He said, "He rejected me too." I felt His arms around me holding me tight as we cried together. It was as though my Daddy and I grieved together over the loss of his child and identified with the pain in both of us.

Perhaps you have never experienced His presence and have never felt His loving arms around you. Maybe you haven't known how to express your heart to God. I am going to ask you to write a letter to God. The following will help you to understand this exercise:

Have you lost a loved one and still feel the pain? Do you have an anger problem? Have you been rejected? Are you carrying unforgiveness, bitterness and resentment? Do you need healing physically, emotionally and spiritually? Are you experiencing depression? Do you have fear of the unknown? Are you burdened with shame and guilt?

If any of these apply to you . . . . tell God about it. He is here to walk through your trials with you.

John 10:4-5 says, "When he has brought his own sheep outside, he walks on before them, and the sheep follow him because they know his voice. They will never (on any account) follow a stranger, but will run away from him because they do not know the voice of strangers or recognize their call." AMP

Before you write your letter to God . . . . say this with me!

Lord, your word says, "I am your sheep and you are my Shepherd." You have walked before me and I follow you because I know your voice. I will never follow a voice of a stranger but will run from him because I do not recognize his call. Thank you for revealing what is on my heart so that I may give it to you. I believe that you have the answer for all of my problems and I wait to hear your wisdom, guidance and direction for my life. In Jesus' Name. Amen.

Now begin writing your letter. If you are alone or in a group setting play some instrumental worship music in the background and take about ten minutes to write your letter. This letter will not be seen by anyone but you and God! Anything that you would like to share afterwards is entirely up to you.

Now that you have written your letter are you ready for God's reply? I believe that prayer is a two way conversation. You talk . . . . God listens! He talks . . . . you listen!

Okay, let's take another 10 minutes to hear God's heart for you and the situation. Continue with the background instrumental worship music. Take out another piece of paper and wait for God to speak to you. Don't get discouraged if you don't hear from Him today. Continue writing and speaking to God daily and wait for Him to write His answer on your heart! One day when I gave this exercise to a group of women on talking and listening for God's voice, some women felt His presence for the first time but didn't hear His voice. Later as they continued spending time with the Lord they began to hear His voice of wisdom for their situations.

As you spend time in His presence daily you may begin to experience visions or dreams. Some of you may receive a word from God telling you to forgive . . . . let go . . . . or trust Him. You may begin to feel His light on the darkness of your heart or receive more hunger for Him.

God may remove stress suddenly that will cause healing physically, emotionally and spiritually. You may receive a word for the future or His words of knowledge and wisdom for your present situation. The turmoil in your life may suddenly dissipate as you feel His peace in the midst of your circumstances. As you spend time listening to His heart you may receive a deliverance of fear, depression or illness. Or you may receive an encouraging word for someone else who is in a hard situation in their life.

Take this time for group discussion for anyone who would like to share what God has written on their heart.

One day a woman was praying for me and was given a vision by the Lord. A demon was standing at the door with his foot holding the door so it could not open the whole way. God showed us that it was a demon of obstruction.

As long as I had this deep pain inside my heart it blocked me from receiving the fullness of God's love and retarded my progress from moving ahead with God's plan for my life.

Refer to both images on page 37 in the book *"Touch Me"*.

Notice in the first image God gave me a revelation of my heart. In the second image God had given me a dream of how we try to change ourselves and walk around with guilt and condemnation because we cannot transform our hearts. Without a relationship with the Lord I would not have received His revelation on the pieces of my heart and would have continued to allow the enemy to heap condemnation on me since I couldn't change myself!

When I began to give those pieces of my heart to the Lord the spirit of advancement came in and kicked out the demon of obstruction. The enemy could no longer impede God's declaration for my life.

Are you dealing with a demon of obstruction or is the spirit of advancement working in your life?

Read Psalm 139:23 (NIV) on page 38 in the book *"Touch Me"*.

Notice the word **"test."** When I first announced this scripture to a women's group it made them cringe inside since they really didn't want to be tested. Remember God never tempts us but He will test us.

A test is a series of questions, problems, etc., intended to measure the extent of knowledge, aptitudes, intelligence and other mental traits and subjection to conditions that disclose the true character of a person or thing in relation to some particular quality. (Funk and Wagnall)

When I was studying to become an insurance agent I had to undergo a lot of tests to receive my licenses. Knowing that I was going to be tested brought a lot of emotions to the surface and my true character came forth in worry, anxiousness and fear.

Eventually by giving these emotions to the Lord, I received all of my licenses and became an insurance agent for thirteen years before God called me to launch Promise Land Ministries in 2003.

I began working for Prudential. Their slogan was, "Do you own a piece of the rock." Later I worked in an office that sold Nationwide that says, "They are on your side." State Farm says, "They are there." All State says, "You are in good hands." The last insurance we sold was Erie whose promise is service.

Do you own a piece of the rock?

I Corinthians 10:4 says, "And they all drank the same spiritual (supernaturally given) drink. For they drank from a spiritual Rock which followed them (produced by the sole power of God Himself without natural instrumentality), and the Rock was Christ."(AMP)

Do you trust that God is on your side?

1 Chronicles 22:18 says, "Is not the Lord your God with you? And has He not given you peace on every side? For He has given the inhabitants of the land into my hand, and the land is subdued before the Lord and His people." (AMP)

Do you believe that you are in good hands?

Psalm 139:10 says, "Even there your hand will guide me, your right hand will hold me fast." (NIV)

Do you feel His presence daily?

Psalm 23:6 says, "Surely or only goodness, mercy, and unfailing love shall follow me all the days of my life, and through the length of my days the house of the Lord (and His presence) shall be my dwelling place." (AMP)

I am reminded when I cooked a deer roast I always placed it in a pan of boiling water on the stove first. When the roast began to boil a film rose to the surface. The longer it cooked the more layers of fat proceeded to reach the surface of the pan. I would take a ladle and begin skimming the fat off the top. Afterwards I would place the roast in a roaster and add carrots, potatoes and onions that would help rid the taste of wild game. If it tasted like a beef roast I would know the process was finished. I knew that it was a success when my family couldn't tell the difference between a deer roast and a beef roast.

When God orders a testing season He places us in a pot of boiling water of our circumstances. In order for us to be more like Jesus we must allow God to remove the impurities in us. As our emotions come to the surface we learn to give them to the Lord so He can purify our hearts. He takes His cup shaped vessel of love and dips out our selfishness, pride, anger, jealousy, and so forth. As our hearts become more purified we become a vessel of honor for our Master's service. With more of the wildness in our hearts removed we grow into maturity in our minds which produce godliness in our character.

Matthew 5:48 says, "You, therefore, must be perfect (growing into complete maturity of godliness in mind and character, having reached the proper height of virtue and integrity), as your heavenly Father is perfect."(AMP)

As I began to ask the Lord to search my heart He showed me areas in my heart that needed to be healed. I began to see Him as my heart and mind specialist and made an appointment with Him daily! As He showed me the broken pieces of my heart, areas that needed extensive surgery and some that needed His medication, I submitted to His plan and purpose for healing me. So began the process of cutting out the deep roots of my heart and mind disease. As I lay in His hospital bed He began to perform a heart and mind transplant.

Refer to the first image on page 39 in the book *"Touch Me"*.

Do you feel like God is pulling, pressing, squeezing and patting you? If so, how are you responding to God?

Refer to the second image on page 39 in the book *"Touch Me"*.

Whether you are in a group setting or by yourself . . . . read this out loud . . . stop . . . . read this again.

Do you feel God touching you?

Pray this with me . . . .

Lord, help me to quiet my heart and mind before you. Thank you for giving me your heart and your spiritual eyes to see what I have not been able to see. Help me to face this deep, deep, deep pain that I have carried for many years.

Read I John 1:5-10 on page 40 in the book *"Touch Me"*.

When God showed me the unforgiveness in my heart towards my dad, I took out a piece of paper and began to list each situation. Then I lifted my list up to the Lord and repeated each one and chose to forgive him.

Perhaps you have unforgiveness in your heart towards a dad, mother, sibling, spouse or other person. You have already asked the Lord to show you what He sees in your heart. As He reveals unforgiveness in your heart He will begin a process of forgiveness if you are willing.

Are you ready for God's revelation? If so, let's begin!

If you are in a group setting or by yourself take out another piece of paper. Play instrumental worship music in the background and begin to write the names of the people and/or the situations that took place in your life that you have either refused or have not been able to forgive. Then lift the list to the Lord and choose to forgive each one you have written. Notice . . . . I said choose. You may not feel like it . . . . that's okay! You do your part in choosing to forgive and God will do His part in changing your heart and freeing you from this pain.

Now you have begun a process of forgiveness. This process will involve a series of actions directed towards a specific aim in choosing to forgive.

It will stretch your faith but as you continually choose forgiveness God will bring it to completion as you continue to surrender this pain to Him. In this process do not allow the enemy to speak discouragement in telling you that you haven't forgiven. God is the heart changer and He knows exactly how and when to change your heart.

Refer to the image on page 41 in the book *"Touch Me"*.

In this process of forgiveness God showed me that garbage was buried inside of me. Because I allowed God to take control of the dark area of unforgiveness in my heart, I began to come up quickly out of the excretion of pain and suffering therefore it was no longer buried.

Read page 42 in the book *"Touch Me"*.

11. I received a miracle when I prayed for my mother and dad? What happened? Are you ready for a miracle?

Read pages 44-47 on forgiveness in the book *"Touch Me"*.

12. What is the definition of forgiveness?

13. When we hold onto offenses what happens to us?

14. What happens when we continue to internalize the offense?

Read Ephesians 4:31-32 on page 45 in the book *"Touch Me"*.

15. When we are offended how should we forgive?

I am learning when I experience an offense to immediately choose to forgive. So . . . . I say, "Lord, I choose to forgive (name the person or situation). I am going to look at the good in my life and allow you to deal with the bad."

16. What doesn't forgiveness mean?

17. What does forgiveness do?

18. Forgiveness lets go of what?

19. Forgiveness does not require what?

Read Matthew 18:21-22 on page 46 in the book *"Touch Me"*.

20.   How often should we forgive?

Matthew 6:12-15 says:

And forgive us our debts, as we also have forgiven (left, remitted, and let go of the debts, and have given up resentment against) our debtors.

And lead (bring) us not into temptation, but deliver us from the evil one. For yours is the kingdom and the power and the glory forever. Amen.

For if you forgive people their trespasses (their reckless and willful sins, leaving them, letting them go, and giving up resentment), your heavenly Father will also forgive you.

But if you do not forgive others their trespasses (their reckless and willful sins, leaving them, letting them go, and giving up resentment), neither will your Father forgive you your trespasses. (AMP)

When we choose to let go of the offense and not allow resentment to enter our heart God delivers us from the evil. When we hold onto the resentment and choose not to forgive we tie God's hands to work in our life and in the life of other persons.

If you forgive the sins of any, they are forgiven them; if you retain the sins of any, they are retained. (John 20:23 NKJ)

When Jesus died on the cross He gave us remission of our sins and cancelled the suffering that we should have to endure that released us from the guilt and penalty of sin. In laying aside His will for the Father's plan of redemption He took all of our sin upon him and gave us a path to follow in His footsteps. A spirit of accusation, lies, condemnation and mockery came through His chosen people yet while suffering in agony Jesus said, "Father forgive them for they know not what they do."

When they got to the place called Skull Hill, they crucified him, along with the criminals, one on his right, the other on his left. Jesus prayed,

"Father, forgive them; they don't know what they're doing." Dividing up his clothes, they threw dice for them. The people stood there staring at Jesus, and the ringleaders made faces, taunting, "He saved others. Let's see him save himself! The Messiah of God . . . ha! The Chosen . . . ha!" (Luke 23:33-34 Message)

Notice Jesus didn't choose to say he forgave because the people said they were sorry or changed their minds. They continued to possess the spirit of mockery and hatred towards him. By speaking words of forgiveness Jesus showed us a plan of letting go of bitterness, resentment, anger and unforgiveness so that it would no longer possess our heart and mind so we could experience His love, peace and joy in the midst of pain and sorrow.

So . . . *let me ask you this question. When you have forgiven the other person will you still remember the offense? Some people say that if you have truly forgiven the offense you won't remember it. So . . . let's talk about what it means to remember.*

And they will no more teach each man his neighbor and each man his brother, saying, "Know the Lord, for they will all know Me [recognize, understand, and be acquainted with Me], from the least of them to the greatest, says the Lord. For I will forgive their iniquity, and I will [seriously] remember their sin no more." (Jeremiah 31:34 AMP)

The Hebrew word for **remember** is *zakar* which means to mention, recount, record and think on. (Strong's)

I am reminded of the Amish families in Lancaster County that experienced horrific deaths of five of their children. The wife of the man who injured and killed those children execution style went through a tremendous grieving of both her husband and what he had become and the senseless death of the Amish children that were their neighbors. The Amish families immediately chose to forgive the woman's husband and actually went to visit her. They told the wife they held no grudges against her and her family and put forgiveness to action by showing them grace, love and mercy in the midst of this tragedy.

They shared the funds with the gunman's family that was raised by many people for the tremendous cost for burials and hospital expenses. The wife and her family were overwhelmed by the power of forgiveness that brought steps to healing they so desperately needed. I'm sure there were many thoughts and emotions that rose up within the Amish family's heart and mind but I believe they had to continually choose to say no to unforgiveness and anger that leads to resentment and bitterness. Will they ever forget the loss they suffered? Of course not! However in choosing to forgive they did not recount or remind the wife of her husband's sin. I believe as they continually chose forgiveness and acted on it God began a process of healing within all of them that led to letting go of the pain that brought them to experience and receive God's love in a greater way!

Forgiveness is God's divine message of love, peace and joy. Without forgiveness we remain captive to the cancer in our soul!

Read and meditate on Matthew 5:23-24 on page 47 in the book *"Touch Me"*.

God is in the ministry of reconciliation however as long as you have made the choice to forgive and have done all that God is calling you to do . . . . there are some exceptions:

- You are not responsible if the other person does not want to reconcile.

- If you have been verbally and emotionally abused and the abuser continues . . . . there will not be a true reconciliation without their admission and repentance of the sin.

- When the other person is deceased even though there was never reconciliation, God will free you of the pain of your past and remove any guilt or condemnation from the enemy.

You cannot change the other person but as you have made the choice to forgive them you have allowed God to change your heart, heal your pain and work in your life and theirs.

Read page 48 and refer to the image in the book *"Touch Me"*.

Perhaps you are going through a separation or divorce right now and you are experiencing intense jealousy. Ask God to help you to look at those involved through God's eyes and separate the sin from the person.

Sometimes we are not aware of jealousy in our heart. One day I found myself upset at something someone had said that I didn't agree with. As I entertained those words in my mind I became angry. I realized something was wrong within me. As I talked with the Lord and expressed this emotion I heard him say, "You are jealous." I was shocked at this word from the Lord and certainly didn't know that I was jealous. So . . . . I said, "Lord, what am I jealous about?" I heard Him say, "You see them as having the perfect life that you have always desired." He told me that from the time I was a little girl all I wanted was a perfect life with a white picket fence around it. As God revealed this darkness in my heart a song began to rise up in my spirit called, "Take my life and let it be." I realized that even though it wasn't my desire or God's for me to experience the pain and suffering of divorce . . . . every moment of my life was set apart for Him and He was using it for my good and His glory. As I repented of the jealousy and gave Him the anger my heart flowed in ceaseless praise for how He had brought me through all these tests and trials in my life.

Feelings of jealousy can move in on us when we least expect them. While I was writing this I asked my husband to portray a character in an upcoming skit that would be presented in two churches. His response was a flat no! Now I've learned that if he says no God may have someone else to portray the character and that enables me to let it go. However, he had portrayed a character for a lady directing a play in our church. My thought was, "You did it for her but not for me." However, I kept my emotions intact and resisted saying anything negative to my husband. Later that night I had a dream involving this lady who had asked my husband to portray the character. She was trying to close a huge garage door and couldn't since it was too heavy. She said, "We don't have the strength with our age so you probably won't be able to close it either." Something happened within me. My adrenaline kicked in and suddenly I had the strength of an ox and pulled that garage door shut! I looked at her with great pride. When I woke up I realized God was showing me something about this situation. I realized my attitude was not healthy since I wanted to show her up. Even though I resisted saying anything to my husband I didn't resist the thoughts! Immediately I chose to forgive my husband for his insensitivity and gave the emotion and gut honesty to the Lord.

Then I took authority over the spirit of jealousy that wanted to control my mind and confessed that I have the mind of Christ. Now I want you to understand that I have nothing against this precious woman and that we are friends. She was totally innocent in all of this. However, God showed me that if I hadn't resisted the thoughts someday something could have triggered my emotions and I could have acted out this behavior towards her. If that would have happened it would have wounded our friendship.

I encourage you to ask the Lord to reveal any hidden thoughts of jealousy within you so you can lay them at Jesus' feet and experience God's freedom in your heart and mind. Is there anyone who triggers thoughts of jealousy when you are around them or hear about them? C'mon get honest with the Lord. If there is, follow those steps that I just mentioned toward freedom in your mind and emotions.

Are you dealing with shame and guilt for something in the past?

If you have already asked the Lord and the person to forgive you do not allow the enemy to keep you bound in shame and guilt any longer. As you ask the Lord to help you to forgive yourself, He will remove the shame and guilt that has been satan's entrapment to keep you from receiving God's love. If you haven't asked for forgiveness and the Holy Spirit is convicting you at this moment ask the Lord to forgive you and help you to forgive yourself. As I repented of the fear of not standing up for the Jewish girl in my class God gave me another chance to make it right with her. When I asked her to forgive me God brought forgiveness and healing to both of us.

Notice when I wept I felt the conviction of the Holy Spirit not the entrapment of guilt and shame from the enemy.

Refer to the image on page 49 in the book ***"Touch Me"***.

Do you feel the enemy continually pecking at your mind with thoughts of what you have done wrong?

One of the girls in the Promise Land Ministries team was having negative thoughts continually pecking at her mind. Suddenly she felt God's presence begin from her head and work down to her feet. She described His healing presence as a car wash.

One day my husband decided to take our vehicle through a car wash in another county. I noticed there were three choices . . . . Express . . . . Super and Ultimate. Express was just a quick work at high speed with no deep cleaning. Super involved excessive cleaning but did not compare to the Ultimate. The Ultimate started with a presoak and proceeded into a deep cleaning including the tires. The final result brought a polished look that shined like a brand new vehicle!

One day as I was spending time in God's presence I heard Him say, "My first commandment is to love me with all of your heart, soul and mind. My second commandment is to love your neighbor as yourself. This is my ultimate makeover for all of my children. When I entered your heart you received my gift of love for eternity. Your inexpressible joy is coming."

Matthew 22:37-39 says, "Jesus replied, Love the Lord your God with all your heart and with all your soul and with all of your mind. This is the first and greatest commandment. And the second is Love your neighbor as yourself." (NIV)

How do we love God or our neighbor if we don't love our self?

Let's take a look at some exceptions that we use:

I love God when He answers my prayers. I love God when I feel His presence. I love God when I receive His blessings. I love God when my life is full of peace, love and joy. I love God when he fits into my plan.

I love my neighbor when they are not nasty or mean. I love my neighbor when they never yell at me. I love my neighbor when they compliment and never criticize me. I love my neighbor when they always encourage me and never bring discouragement. I love my neighbor when they never gossip about me. I love my neighbor when they are never jealous over me.

Welcome and receive (to your hearts) one another, then, even as Christ has welcomed and received you, for the glory of God. (Romans 15:7 AMP)

Notice it says receive them to your heart.

1 John 4:20 says, "If anyone says, I love God, and hates (detests, abominates) his brother (in Christ), he is a liar; for he who does not love his brother, whom he has seen, cannot love God, Whom he has not seen." (AMP)

So how do we love the unlovely and not retaliate? How do we get our focus off ourselves and onto God?

God has an ultimate makeover that begins with soaking in His presence that leads to His excessive cleaning in all areas of your heart and mind. This process of holiness leads to true happiness. As he polishes the dullness within us it produces His final result in becoming a reflection of Jesus that brings joy that is incapable of being expressed or put into words.

One morning the Lord spoke this in my heart. "As a tea bag continues to make the tea stronger as it steeps, so I desire for you to be steeped in my presence. When you are steeped in my presence I give you my strength for your weaknesses. Come, my child. Let me steep you in my love, peace and joy!"

When the dry leaves in the tea bag saturate the liquid it takes on the flavor of the dry ingredient. As we steep in God's presence daily we begin to savor His flavor and experience the sweetness of His fruit of love, joy and peace.

Song of Solomon 2:3 says, "Like an apple tree among the trees of the wood, so is my beloved (shepherd) among the sons (cried the girl)! Under His shadow I delighted to sit, and His fruit was sweet to my taste." (AMP)

Do you delight to sit in His presence?

Have you tasted his sweet fruit of peace, love and joy?

In the beginning of the separation in my first marriage a woman gave me this word from the Lord. "Happiness is coming to you . . . . more than you have ever had." I thought that meant reconciliation in my marriage. When that didn't take place, I kept looking for other happiness. Then one day God spoke this in my heart, "In holiness there is happiness. In happiness there is holiness. I have come to give you the happiness you have waited for. Many of my people do not recognize what true happiness is.

I will show you more of my holiness that will bring you the happiness I promised many years ago."

As I was further into this process of healing God began to show me that true happiness is the holiness. As I embraced the trials and tests in my life, instead of running I began to experience the promises God desires for me.

Refer to the image on page 50 in the book ***"Touch Me"***.

Do you feel hardness in your heart or God's Drano of love penetrating the hardness?

When a drain becomes clogged it is annoying and may disrupt your meal preparation for company. Depending on how serious the clog is, you may have to cease preparing a lovely meal and settle for take outs!

When your heart is clogged it can be very annoying and disrupt your everyday activities. One moment you can be laughing and having a great day when suddenly a stressful circumstance triggers bitterness and causes you to explode in anger. When you give the bitterness to God and choose to forgive, tough clogs don't stand a chance with God's Drano of love! His Drano attacks clogs that others can't reach.

One day I was praying with a lady. God gave me a vision of dirty laundry piling up on her. When laundry is dirty it can produce very bad odors. God had me actually place many pieces of laundry on her for her to see the true picture of what she was allowing into her life. She repented of becoming an enabler and asked the Lord to give her the boldness needed to change her life.

Perhaps you are allowing a loved one to pile their dirty laundry on you. In other words you have become an enabler. People that have an addiction whether it's drugs, alcohol, sex, or food will not take the responsibility for their actions or words as long as they can depend on you to bail them out! They can only be helped when they are made accountable. The enemy will use their weaknesses that bring words of guilt and condemnation to penetrate your weaknesses. When you give those weaknesses to God he will give you the strength and courage needed to stand up to this evil which will bring them into accountability and allow God to change their heart and mind.

Perhaps you are listening to condemning thoughts in your mind from the enemy that is an irrational belief about yourself or what you should or should not have done. In my first marriage the enemy bombarded my mind with thoughts of condemnation and guilt for not being able to help my husband to change which led me on a path to destruction until the Lord intervened.

So far in this chapter we have discussed three entrances the enemy uses to keep us bound in guilt and condemnation. So, let's take a look at the fourth entrance . . . . unconfessed sin.

Read page 51 and refer to Psalm 32:3-4 in the book ***"Touch Me"***.

God's hand was heavy upon David who caused him to suffer emotionally, physically and spiritually. Finally God revealed the unconfessed sin of David through his prophet Nathan. When David confessed the adultery with Bathsheba and the murder of her husband Uriah there were consequences however, God immediately forgave him. If David would not have repented and confessed the sin before God and Nathan he would never have been set free of the bondage of guilt and condemnation and would have continued his life in misery. When we see people's sin we may discard them out of our lives however, God never discards His children. He is always waiting on us to confess and repent of the sin and is willing to forgive us immediately.

And David said to Nathan, "I have sinned against the Lord." And Nathan said to David, "The Lord also has put away your sin; you shall not die." (II Samuel 12:13 AMP)

Are you dealing with any of these entrances to guilt?

- Confessed sin that God has forgiven but you haven't forgiven yourself.

- Guilt inflicted on you by others' condemnation.

- Self-inflicted guilt

- Unconfessed sin.

If you have unconfessed sin please meet with someone that you know you can trust not to let others know and confess to them before God so you too can be set free of this bondage!

As long as you don't confess the sin you will continue to possess it. When you confess the sin you will no longer possess it!

Unconfessed sin keeps you in bondage and allows the enemy to speak his words of condemnation. Confessed sin brings freedom and allows you to hear God's truth and receive His love for you.

If you are in a group setting divide into groups of two and pray for each other. One person confesses the guilt and repents and gives it to the Lord verbally. The other person prays for her or him. If you are by yourself imagine yourself holding God's hand while you confess and repent of the guilt and give it to the Lord. Jesus has been your intercessor and is still making intercession for you right now!

Read page 52 in the book ***"Touch Me"***.

21.   What can you do to stay free of developing a root of unforgiveness?

Refer to the image on page 52 in the book ***"Touch Me"***.

Are you allowing God to cleanse every area of your life?

Refer to the first two images on page 53 in the book ***"Touch Me"***.

A master, guide and director have this is common . . . . they all have authority over something or someone!

Have you given God the authority over you and all of your circumstances?

If you haven't . . . . what areas of your life are you still directing?

Refer to the last image on page 53 in the book ***"Touch Me"***.

Perhaps you have a tangled mess that has brought pain and suffering for many years. Are you ready to allow God to unravel the mess?

Read pages 54-56 and refer to the image on page 54 in the book ***"Touch Me"***.

Are you willing to lay hold of the siege and render satan's power ineffective in your life? If so, please take four pieces of paper and title the first one . . . Painful scenes in my mind.

Title the second one . . . . hurtful words spoken over me. Title the third one . . . . actions of others that grieved me. Last but not least title the fourth one . . . . thoughts of the past, present, and future that plague me.

Now, pray this prayer with me.

Lord, thank you for revealing the siege that has been in my mind. I ask you to recall every painful scene, hurtful words that have been spoken over me and about me, actions of others that have grieved me and thoughts of the past, present and future that have plagued me. Thank you for beginning this process of rendering satan's power ineffective over my life. In Jesus' Name. Amen.

Play instrumental music in the background and allow the Holy Spirit to reveal what you need to write down. Take about ten minutes to listen and write what you hear in the spirit. Don't be concerned if you can't think of them all right now. This is the beginning of a continuation that the Holy Spirit will show you in His time.

Jenny Hagemeyer

As you sit in God's presence daily, He will unveil any stronghold that has been holding you captive by the enemy. When you acknowledge God's truth, you will experience freedom and healing in your mind and His fortress will surround and protect your heart and mind.

Daring

This chapter brings the entrance of God's word that brings light onto our paths!

Your word is a lamp to my feet and a light to my path. (Psalm 119:105 AMP)

In my first marriage we had a cabin in the woods. When it was newly built we did not have a bathroom and had to go outside to use an outhouse. I always dreaded going outside in the dark. However, I felt safer with a flash light that illuminated my path. I was able to see any wild animals such as bears, skunks or a fox on my path when the light was shining. With the light shining I could stay on the right path and not get into high grass where snakes would make their nest. My fear began to dissipate as long as I had the source of light. With the light I could reach my destination and also find my way back to the cabin.

God's word is our source of light. It guides us onto the right path, teaches us about the enemy's tactics, reveals any danger in our lives, removes fear, worry and anxiety and helps us to reach the destination that God is calling us to.

The word lamp is taken from the Hebrew word that means to glisten. (Strong's)

The word light is taken from the Hebrew word that means illumination, happiness, or bright and clear. (Strong's)

One wintry morning I was looking out my dining room window as I was working on the computer. The snow that had fallen during the night covered our deck. As I caught a glimpse of the sunshine on the new fallen snow it seemed to glisten. At that moment the Lord showed me a picture of my heart.

It too was glistening with the Sonshine of God's love upon me with peace, love and joy as I have made the choice to spend time daily in His presence and to study His word. I could feel the happiness within my heart and began to praise Him for showing me His illumination and giving me His divine revelation! I realized after many years of allowing God to heal my heart and meditating in His word my heart was healthy and happy! A healthy heart is a happy heart.

What does God see in your heart? Is it healthy and happy or diseased and miserable?

The Lord began to heal my heart of the years of pain and suffering as I communed with Him and allowed Him to illuminate my heart and reveal the dark areas that I was not aware of.

Read Isaiah 55:11 on page 57 in the book *"Touch Me"*.

Are you reading God's word daily and allowing Him to produce healing in your heart and to accomplish His purpose for your life?

Refer to both images on page 58 in the book *"Touch Me"*.

1.   When you allow yourself to entertain thoughts of negativity you feed your flesh with what?

2.   How do you feed your spirit?

Are you feeding your flesh or your spirit?

But I say walk and live (habitually) in the (Holy) Spirit (responsive to and controlled and guided by the Spirit); then you will certainly not gratify the cravings and desires of the flesh (of human nature without God). (Galatians 5:16 AMP)

Read page 59 and refer to image in the book *"Touch Me"*.

God places His tray of goodness, mercy and love before us daily.

Surely or only goodness, mercy, and unfailing love shall follow me all the days of my life, and through the length of my days the house of the Lord (and His presence) shall be my dwelling place. (Psalm 23:6 AMP)

Satan entices God's creation with his hidden evil, mercilessness and hatred that eventually brings death to your body, soul and spirit when you yield to his temptations.

This (evil) persuasion is not from Him who called you (Who invited you to freedom in Christ). (Galatians 5:8 AMP)

Read page 60 and refer to Job 36:16 in the book ***"Touch Me"***.

Are you going through an affliction that has placed you into a restriction (limited or confined)?

Are you sitting in a dark room of negativity and catering to your flesh?

Do you dare to take God at His word for all your circumstances in your life?

But Jesus looked at them and said, "With men this is impossible, but all things are possible with God." (Matthew 19:26 AMP)

Behold, I am the Lord, the God of all flesh; is there anything too hard for me? (Jeremiah 32:27AMP)

But without faith it is impossible to please and be satisfactory to Him. For whoever would come near to God must (necessarily) believe that God exists and that He is the rewarder of those who earnestly and diligently seek Him (out). (Hebrews 11:6 AMP)

At midnight on September 2, 2009 our daughter and her family suddenly lost their home. We received a call from her at 12:15 AM and through her tears she communicated the details of her situation. A fire had suddenly ripped through a six family dwelling complex that left twelve people homeless and a total loss of everything they owned. No one had renter's insurance coverage. As the days went by the fire was declared arson!

Praise God! No one was burned or even had any smoke inhalation. My husband immediately left for Eastern Pennsylvania with a great heaviness in his heart and many questions in his mind. What would happen now? Where would our daughter, son-in-law, and three grandchildren, ages fifteen, nine and seven months old live? How could they ever put the pieces of their lives back together again?

Where do you go when there are no answers and you can't make sense of anything that is happening? When you are plagued with a long term illness that leaves you experiencing pain in your body daily?

When your spouse decides he/she doesn't love you anymore and the marriage is over? When you had a job of twenty five years and suddenly the plant closes and you don't have enough years to retire? When you are gripped with fear as you hear the horror stories all around you?

How do you leave the seat of the 3D's of discouragement, despair and depression and cross over to the 3R's . . . . relationship, renewal and refreshment?

I believe the greatest threat to the enemy's kingdom is an <u>intimate personal relationship</u> with our Father. As you spend time in the presence of an Almighty God you will begin to experience His <u>renewal</u> in your heart and mind that leads to <u>refreshment</u> in your soul!

The evening following the fire our ministry team met in our home for our weekly meeting. We had many other prayer requests that included illnesses, job loss, financial hardships, marriage problems, and people filled with fear, worry and anxiousness. Two days before our meeting I had written scriptures down that I believed God had directed me to not only read and meditate on but to confess over all our situations.

Here are six scriptures that we read, meditated on and confessed with our mouth.

I love You fervently and devotedly, O Lord, my Strength. The Lord is my Rock, my Fortress, and my Deliverer; my God, my keen and firm Strength in Whom I will trust and take refuge, my Shield, and the Horn

of my salvation, my High Tower. I will call upon the Lord, Who is to be praised; so shall I be saved from my enemies. (Psalm 18:1-3 AMP)

We began telling the Lord how much we loved and adored Him. We lifted up our praises to Him for who He is! We not only called Him our rock, fortress and our deliverer but we really trusted that He is. Even though our flesh wanted to run with our emotions we ran to our refuge, shield and High Tower. We thanked Him that He would save us from the enemy of our souls.

O taste and see that the Lord (our God) is good! Blessed (happy, fortunate, to be envied) is the man who trusts and takes refuge in Him. (Psalm 34:8AMP)

As we worshipped Him in spirit and in the truth of His word we felt His presence surround us and began to recall the goodness of the Lord in our prayers of the past.

And be not conformed to this world, but be transformed . . . (changed by the entire renewal of your mind by its ideals and new attitudes by the renewing of your mind, that you may prove what is that good, acceptable and perfect will of God. (Romans 12:2 AMP)

We knew that we could not allow our minds to wander into satan's trap of negativity. Therefore, as we confessed His word over all of these people and situations our minds were renewed with God's word of truth which led us to new mindsets and attitudes of peace and joy.

For God did not give us a spirit of timidity (of cowardice, of craven and cringing and fawning fear), but (He has given us a spirit) of power and of love and of calm and well-balanced mind and discipline and self-control. (II Timothy 1:7 AMP)

As we placed the fear of the future in the Lord's hands we began to experience His faith rising up in our spirits. His spirit of power and love and a calm mind brought the opportunity for God to show Himself strong!

Lean on, trust in, and be confident in the Lord with all your heart and mind and do not rely on your own insight or understanding. In all your

ways know, recognize, and acknowledge Him, and He will direct and make straight and plain your paths. (Proverbs 3:5-6 AMP)

As we leaned on and were confident in the Lord we were not relying on our own understanding or insight. We had to stop trying to figure everything out and put our focus on Him. After all, how could we understand all the devastating things that were going on in our families? We knew that we could not find a path on our own to change this course so we believed that God would direct and make the path clear that was needed to be taken to begin restoration.

The last scripture we confessed was **"Yet amid all these things we are more than conquerors and gain a surpassing victory through Him who loved us." (Romans 8:37 AMP)**

As we were praying this scripture I had a vision of a football being thrown into the air and on it was written "You are more than a conqueror." Jesus is your offense to help you score in the game of life and also your defense against the enemy. He has a surpassing Victory for you and will defeat the enemy of discouragement.

Surpassing means to go beyond or past in degree or amount; to go beyond the reach or powers of; exceeding. (Funk and Wagnall)

Victory refers to the final defeat of an enemy or opponent: "Victory at all costs, victory in spite of all terror, victory however long and hard the road may be" (Winston S. Churchill).

Victory is to the over comer; it is not something that comes to you automatically or without effort. You have to seize it and take it by force. It is success in the struggle. Do not take the position of a powerless victim. God has called you to be an over comer, conqueror and triumphant in all things. Refuse to allow the enemy to victimize you. Rise up and take your rightful position! You are a child of the Most High God!!

I'm sure that most of you have memorized these scriptures as children. However, these six scriptures in their simplicity are very powerful and profound for every day whether we are experiencing valleys or mountain tops in our life.

So if I may…I would like to tell you the rest of the story.

Within one week our daughter and her family were no longer homeless. With the help of many churches and families, everything they needed to set up housekeeping was supplied. Clothing for everyone was donated from all counties. Our daughter located another house to rent and a team of many wonderful people gathered together to move them in. God moved in the hearts of many people to not only bless our family but also the other people who were involved in the fire. God accomplished the impossible! He went beyond and superseded what the enemy meant for evil and brought a victory in all of their lives. What an awesome God He is!

One month before this took place I had been running an errand for a friend. As I was driving I picked up my cell phone and called her to ask a question. Suddenly my van swerved off the road and onto the side. There was a stone wall along the side that I should have crashed into. However, within a split second I was driving on a path with high brush all around me. As quickly as I swerved off the road I was no longer on the path but back on the road again. Amazingly I had no fear during this ordeal. Afterwards, I stopped to see the damage done to our van since I felt sure there would be deep scratches, however there were none! At that moment the Holy Spirit spoke to me. He said, "What seemed like a tragedy I have turned for my glory. Look for me to do the impossible!" What's more amazing is I have not been able to find the path I was on. It seems like it doesn't exist yet God in His mercy took me onto His path of safety and brought me back with more wonder and amazement of Him.

Again with the devastation of the fire, God turned what seemed to be a tragedy into His glory!

Now I can hear some of you saying, "Okay, that's great for everyone else. However, my situation hasn't changed. I am still waiting on God."

We don't understand God's timing but we need to dare to take God at His word. One day I was talking to the Lord. I knew what He had spoken to me years ago concerning a particular situation. I still had not seen it manifest so I asked the Lord if there was anything I was doing to prevent what He had spoken to me from happening. He said, "I am doing my greatest work in you now." At first I didn't understand until He said, "I am taking you into a deeper trust in me." Was I going to trust Him even when nothing was happening?

So . . . . here is the test. Do you trust Him even when nothing is happening and you see no answers to your prayers?

I'd like to encourage you to read, meditate, memorize and confess the six scriptures above as a part of your daily devotions with the Lord and watch what He does in, through and for you as you agree with His word for your life.

Read the story of my umbrella heist on pages 60-61 in the book *"Touch Me"*.

The morning that my umbrella was missing I told one of my friends at church. She said, "Jenny, knowing you God probably wants to teach you something to teach others." Immediately, my attitude changed from being disgusted and I asked the Lord what He had in mind. In this lesson God revealed to me how He sees us in our imperfection yet loves us with His amazing perfect love.

Read Psalm 17:8 on page 60 in the book *"Touch Me"*.

The meaning of the "apple of my eye" is a person that is greatly loved, treasured and adored. Parents . . . . just as you look at your children as the "apple of your eye", your Father sees you as the "apple of His eye!" In other words you are an expression of God's love!

God created man in His own image. In the image of God He created him. Male and female He created them. (Genesis 1:27)

I am reminded of how I love to watch an artist begin his painting. In the beginning he starts out with all kinds of brush strokes that don't look like anything special. However, as he continues adding more short and long strokes it begins to take on a look that is intriguing. As he fills in the areas that are needed with more colors it begins to have character and begins to look like a work of art. Finally, when the painting is finished it becomes a masterpiece that is an expression of the artist!

You are a hand crafted work of art made by the Master Craftsman!

Do you see yourself as an expression of God's love? If not, how do you see yourself?

When I compared the two umbrellas I looked at their performance and appearance which brought judgment and criticism. God does not look at our good works and appearance. Because of Jesus death and resurrection we are hidden behind the cross. When we ask Jesus into our heart God sees the righteousness of Jesus and we become the "apple of His eye!"

For our sake He made Christ (virtually) to be sin who knew no sin, so that in and through Him we might become (endued with, viewed as being in, and examples of) the righteousness of God (what we ought to be, approved and acceptable and in right relationship with Him, by His goodness). (II Corinthians 5:21 AMP)

Refer to image on page 62 in the book *"Touch Me"*.

God didn't create us to be angels but created us with weaknesses to give to Him so He could perfect them.

Think of this! When we strive for perfection we become disillusioned and discouraged since we will never be able to attain perfection in this life. However, when we give these weaknesses to the Lord He does in us what we can't do for ourselves!

When God spoke this to me I felt like a huge boulder was removed from my shoulders. As I have been learning to give all of my weaknesses to Him I have been experiencing more of the freedom that God has intended for us and I no longer pursue perfection but the reflection of Jesus!

Are you pursuing perfection or reflection?

Is your focus on your appearance or God's appearance?

Jesus freed us from self-examination and from examining other people that don't measure up to our standards!

Fred and I and the Promise Land Ministries team along with their husbands were preparing for a renewal during a Sunday morning church service. As I was seeking the Lord for His wisdom and direction I heard the words, "About Face" in my spirit. The Lord showed me a vision of soldiers standing at attention before their Commander-in-Chief. However, they didn't look like soldiers that we would normally expect to see. Their shirts were hanging out, spots were on their uniforms, and they were facing the wrong direction. One soldier was even running late. The drill sergeant was so frustrated with them that he began to give orders with harsh words. To make matters worse, as the Commander-in-Chief was waiting for inspection, the soldiers were conducting their own inspections through harsh and critical words with each other. One soldier carried a tide stick to clean another soldier's shirt. This became a drama that we portrayed with a theme of "It's time to face the enemy!"

As soldiers have to face their Commander-in-Chief for inspection daily, we must allow our Commander-in-Chief to examine us daily to reveal the enemy of our soul. Fred and I attended our son's graduation from the fire academy.

One of the speakers said, "To know one's self you must know the enemy!" A Fireman's enemy is fire. However, they must face the fears within before they are able to face the fire.

God's presence dissipates the judgment and critical attitudes of our thinking and behaviors toward one another. He is our heart mender, heart changer and heart mover. Now, we no longer examine ourselves or each other!

One day during one of Reverend Carpenter's messages in a revival in his church he said, "The Holy Spirit doesn't come to rent a room."

When we rent a home it is not ours since it hasn't been bought and paid for. Jesus paid the price and bought us back from the clutches of the enemy when He died on the cross to save us from our sin. When you asked Jesus into your heart He didn't obtain temporary possession of you. He wants full possession in every area of your soul, body and spirit! The Holy Spirit came into you to take up residence in your heart that you might move and have His being.

Do you not know that your body is the temple (the very sanctuary) of the Holy Spirit who lives within you, whom you have received (as a Gift) from God? You are not your own, you were bought with a price (purchased with a preciousness and paid for, made His own). So then, honor God and bring glory to Him in your body. (I Corinthians 6:19-20 AMP)

So . . . "Is the Holy Spirit officially present in your heart or is He just renting a room?"

Refer to the image on page 63 in the book *"Touch Me"*.

Think of this! The same power that raised Jesus from the dead came into you when you asked Jesus into your heart!

As I am typing this I am reminded to check my battery on my lap top and make sure that I don't end up with a dead battery. When the battery starts getting low I must make the choice to plug into the power source. We must make the choice daily to plug into God's power source and get recharged with His vigorous and life-giving force.

Do you recognize the resurrection power that is within you?

Does your spirit feel charged with His power to resist the devil's schemes?

Are you filled with His joy?

And the disciples were continually filled (throughout their souls) with joy and the Holy Spirit. (Acts 13:52 AMP)

This scripture doesn't say sometimes they were filled with joy and the Holy Spirit. They were being renewed every time they plugged into God's power source that helped them endure the trials and tests, persevere in the midst of persecution, stand on God's word against the enemy of discouragement and experience joy in the face of sorrow.

If you have answered no to these last three questions, pray this with me.

Holy Spirit I give you full residence in every area of my body, soul and spirit. I no longer want to do business as usual but need your Holy Spirit to reveal your power within my heart. I need to be recharged by your Spirit. Help me to recognize your power within me. Every area in me that has been dead I ask you to turn on the light of your spirit so that I may live, walk and breathe in your spirit. In Jesus' Name. Amen.

So he said to me, "This is the word of the LORD to Zerubbabel: 'Not by might nor by power, but by my Spirit,' says the LORD Almighty. (Zechariah 4:6 NIV)

Read pages 64-65 and refer to II Corinthians 3:18 in the book *"Touch Me"*.

How do you reflect Jesus when you are going through a trial?

When a trial comes into our life we can choose to hold onto God's hand in the midst of the pain and suffering or we can choose to be bitter and angry at the Lord and let go of His hand! When we choose to give the anger to the Lord and allow Him to heal the pain within our hearts He takes us through the valleys of sorrow and up to the mountain of His joy!

One of the ladies in our team experienced extreme sorrow within one year. She had been pregnant three times and lost every one of her babies during pregnancy. The emotional pain within her was so great that she could hardly bear it.

She experienced anger, frustration, confusion, and discouragement. She openly expressed her emotions. She decided to make the right choices and not hold anger and unforgiveness towards God. She chose to let go of the anger and ask His forgiveness. She began to thank God for her husband and her two daughters and for all the blessings that God had given her. We watched this beautiful young woman become God's joyful child who could have sunk into despondency had she not responded to God's love.

Another beautiful young woman in our team experienced the loss of her three year old who had a malignant brain tumor. Before her little boy's illness God answered two prayers for her. She wanted to spend more time with her children and more time with God. In the midst of making the right choices to not allow bitterness into her soul she had many experiences with the Lord that carried her through the sorrow in her heart. She was able to spend those days with her precious son and daughter. Many people's hearts were changed throughout our community and some accepted Jesus into their heart. The other woman that I spoke of losing three babies earlier became a Christian when she saw the radiance of Jesus in this woman, her sister and the rest of her family. God eventually brought these women into Promise Land Ministries to be used as His vessels to testify of His great love! What an awesome God!

We have no idea how God will use the radiance of Jesus within us to impact the lives of others. Perhaps as you have read these testimonies you too have lost your precious child either in pregnancy, birth or illness. Maybe you have carried this anger for many years and haven't been able to feel God's love and have sunk into a sea of despondency. Some of you may not even recognize anger towards God . . . . after all you are a Christian. Maybe some of you have stuffed the anger and have justified your feelings since God did not answer your prayers. God is here to unlock the darkness within your heart. Will you open up your heart and allow His light to shine today? If so, please pray this with me.

Lord, I am so sorry that I have blamed you for my child's (name him or her) death or illness and I ask for your forgiveness. I confess this anger that I have (stuffed, not recognized or held against you). I don't want to live another day in this despondency or darkness in my soul. I ask that you shine your light on this darkness and remove this pain within my heart and mind that has caused a stronghold in my life. Thank you for allowing me to feel your love that I desperately have needed.

I will testify of your great love and I will tell of all you have done in my life. You have sent your word and healed me from this destruction. In Jesus' Name. Amen

Read pages 66-67 up to the image on page 67 in the book *"Touch Me"*.

3.   What is involved in **STRIFE?**

One day when my children were young teens they got into an argument and were fighting against each other. As I spoke to them to stop fighting I received this vision. I saw small demons laughing and jumping up and down on the bed. The demons laughed with greater intensity as my children continued to fight one another. I realized when we fight against each other the attention is on ourselves and not on God who helps us fight the enemy of our soul.

Finally, be strong in the Lord and in his mighty power. Put on the full armor of God so that you can take your stand against the devil's schemes. For our struggle is not against flesh and blood, but against the rulers, against the authorities, against the powers of this dark world and against the spiritual forces of evil in the heavenly realms. Therefore put on the full armor of God, so that when the day of evil comes, you may be able to stand your ground, and after you have done everything, to stand. Stand firm then, with the belt of truth buckled around your waist, with the breastplate of righteousness in place, and with your feet fitted with the readiness that comes from the gospel of peace. In addition to all this, take up the shield of faith, with which you can extinguish all the flaming arrows of the evil one. Take the helmet of salvation and the sword of the Spirit, which is the word of God. And pray in the Spirit on all occasions with all kinds of prayers and requests. With this in mind, be alert and always keep on praying for all the saints. (Ephesians 6:10-18 NIV)

As long as we are fighting with each other satan continues to throw his flaming arrows and cheers us on. We must continually stand firm with the belt of God's truth of whom we are in the Lord and who He is. We must put on our breastplate of righteousness which is the practical application of truth and put on the shield of our faith in God and believe and obey His word.

We must also put on our helmet of salvation that guards our thoughts and face the enemy with the sword of the spirit which is the word of God and allow God to examine our heart and mind. Then we will be prepared to go wherever the Spirit of the Lord leads us with His peace and become the Army of the Lord standing ready to fight the enemy of our soul!

Every day we need to put on the Armor of God. So . . . . I am going to ask you to do this spiritual exercise with me. Please stand and confess this:

Today I will triumph in the battle of life because I am not ignorant of satan's devices. Therefore, I put on the whole armor of God that is my lifestyle for every day. As I place the **belt of truth** (act as though you are placing a belt around your waist) on me it confiscates the lies from the enemy and frees me from satan's plot for my life. The **breastplate of righteousness** (act as though you are placing this on your chest) brings me the security of who I am in the Lord and who God is! When I place the **helmet of salvation** on (act as though you are placing a helmet on your head) it protects my mind against satan's attacks of negativity and reminds me that God is my hope of salvation that anchors my soul. I take my **shield of faith** (act as though you have a shield in your hand) that defends me from the enemy and helps me to be an over comer. It reminds me that greater is He that is in me than he that is in the world. I abide, confess and take the **living sword of the spirit** (hold up your Bible) which is the word of God that discerns my thoughts and intentions, gives me power to live a victorious life, exposes the enemy's kingdom and enables me to see through God's supernatural vision. Finally, because I have been in **preparation** before going into battle I have received God's **peace** and am ready to tell others of His plan of redemption for us wherever He calls me.

Refer to image on page 67 in the book *"Touch Me"*.

When I attacked my husband's character, automatically I expressed an act that revealed my feelings and attitude because of my past wounds. At that point I had not realized that there were weaknesses in me that were causing me to react instead of respond. God began to deal with me on the difference of reacting and responding! As He showed me the hidden pain within my heart and mind and healed those areas He began to teach me how to respond in love.

When you react you allow the anger to take control instead of giving the Holy Spirit complete control of your heart and mind. When you react by hurling hurtful words back to the other person more harmful words come back to you like a boomerang. Then a game of tit for tat begins and you repay evil with evil.

Do not let yourself be overcome by evil, but overcome (master) evil with good. (Romans 12:21 AMP)

So . . . how do we stop reacting to our spouse or others' hurtful words and respond in love?

Refer to the first image on page 68 in the book *"Touch Me"*.

Read and Meditate on Proverbs 25:11, Isaiah 50:4 and Proverbs 27:19 on page 68 in the book *"Touch Me"*.

In the first scripture I envision gold and silver that is very shiny when it is polished. No matter where you place them . . . they always stand out! This is how God wants our speech to be. No matter where we are our speech should be polished by the Lord so we can stand out as Christians with His words to others.

The second scripture says the Lord has given us a tongue of a disciple and one who is taught. If we don't get into the position of being taught by the Lord we will continue wounding ourselves and others.

The third scripture says when we look into the water we see ourselves. When Jesus looks into your heart does He see His reflection or yours?

As I spent more time in the presence of the Lord and asked Him to reveal the darkness in my heart and root out the pain in me, I began to learn how to respond instead of react. As I chose to humble myself before the Lord and give my husband the mercy and kindness God gives me daily, the Holy Spirit showed me when to remain quiet, when to speak and what to speak. When I meditated on His word that brings life to my spirit I began to speak life into my husband's spirit. I am learning to give my emotions to the Lord so I do not spew out hurtful words to my husband or other people.

He has showed you, O man, what is good. And what does the Lord require of you but to do justly, and to love kindness and mercy, and to humble yourself and walk humbly with your God? (Micah 6:8 AMP)

Satan will try to catch us off guard if we are not regularly spending time with the Lord. As we spend time in the Lord's presence and read and meditate on His word, He will change what we cannot change in our heart and mind.

Are you attending God's classes regularly or are you periodically cutting class?

Are you responding to your spouse and others or are you reacting out of your wounds?

I am learning to say, "Lord, I'm not talking if you aren't talking. You shut the mouth of the lions so they could not harm Daniel. Shut my mouth so I will not harm others with my words."

Refer to the 2ⁿᵈ image on page 68 in the book *"Touch Me"*.

I don't believe that we can light a fire in the heart of God's children if our hearts are not burning for Jesus. Remember the first scripture that we used to increase our faith to believe for those miracles? The first part of **Psalm 18:1 says, "I love you fervently and devotedly."**

Fervently means hot and burning; moved by or showing great intensity; as of emotion or enthusiasm. (Funk and Wagnall)

I am reminded of the candlelight service at the end of our Christmas program in our church. The lights are turned out and everyone holds a candle that hasn't been lit which causes us to remain in the darkness. Then someone begins the process of lighting another person's candle. It carries the whole way down each pew until all the candles are aglow, dispelling the darkness. In this process I have always felt the presence of the Holy Spirit and am moved with great intensity of passion for God.

Never lag in zeal and in earnest endeavor; be aglow and burning with the Spirit, serving the Lord. (Romans 12:11 AMP)

I believe every one of us has a passion for something or someone. But is God your first passion? My husband has a passion for sprint car races that keep him attending them in all kinds of weather. He takes his special seats with backs on them for comfortable seating and places them on the bleachers. With great expectancy he waits for the flag to come down to start the race. Sometimes it will rain before the race begins and the race is delayed until they are able to get the dirt track in shape for racing. This will sometimes cause hours of delay in which he comes home much later than usual. However, he still gets excited over going to the races and has been attending them since he was a little boy. The thrill of not knowing who will win and what is new with all the drivers keeps Fred attending whenever our schedule permits it. C'mon race fans you know what I am talking about! Every Thursday a racing paper arrives and Fred can hardly wait to open up the mail to read the latest news on racing. When Fred relays the events of the race to other men I can see the excitement welling up in their spirits. I see them looking at their wives with pleading eyes while they make plans to attend the races together.

On the other hand I do not enjoy sitting at the races on hot sultry or chilly days. Since the tracks are dry and dusty they must take the time before the race begins to put water on the track so it gives better traction for the race cars. However I still am covered with dirt from head to toe from the dust. Therefore, I do not appreciate getting dirt all through my clothing and hair. When a rain shower comes it will cause the races to be delayed for hours which results in me coming home to shower late at night or early in the morning. When the racing paper arrives I don't even read the front cover. I'm just not interested in who won or who raced who? When I meet with my girlfriends I certainly do not waste my time talking about things I'm not interested in. Racing is not my passion! There is no thrill for me!

When we have a passion for God we will have the excitement of sitting in His presence daily waiting expectantly to hear His voice. When God calls us to go into undesirable places in all kinds of weather conditions we will obey because we love Him. If things don't meet our expectations we learn to give our expectations to God and allow Him to place His expectation in our hearts. When we get up in the morning we can't wait to open God's love letter in anticipation of what God wants to say. We experience His living water on our dry and dusty soul that connects us to His heart! We experience the thrill of His spoken and written word for our circumstances.

As we see God's hand in our life we relay those events with excitement to other people. They become testimonials for the Lord and bring Him all the praise and glory for what He has accomplished in our life. As others see the love of Jesus within us they too want to experience more of Him.

So . . . do you have a passion for God and experience His living water daily or are you feeling dry and parched?

Do you have the excitement of sitting in His presence, daily waiting expectantly to hear His voice or do you feel He will never speak to you?

Do you go out to the place God calls you in all kinds of weather conditions or do you make excuses not to go?

Have you given the Lord your expectations and allowed Him to place His expectations in your heart or are you holding onto yours?

Do you get up in the morning with anticipation of what God's love letter says to you or do you feel disinterested in reading His word?

Have you experienced the thrill of God's written and spoken word for your circumstances or have you allowed your circumstances to steal your joy and take control of you?

Do you relay the events of what God has done for you, in you and through you to others or do you feel God has let you down?

Do other people want their life to change because they see Jesus in you or are you still taking control of your own life?

When our spirit is connected to the Holy Spirit it ignites a flame of passion and enables us to receive the calling God has given us.

But seek ye first the kingdom of God, and his righteousness; and all these things shall be added unto you. (Matthew 6:33 KJ)

Some of you may be saying I had passion for God when I first became saved but I have lost it along the way with disappointments in my life. Some of you may feel that you have disappointed God and it's too late to have a relationship with God. If I may, I'd like to encourage you to pray this with me.

Lord, I feel parched and dry and have not experienced your living water in a long time. I confess that I have not been waiting expectantly for you to speak to me since I have believed that you won't. I have held onto my expectations of how I think my life should be and now I give you my expectations. I ask that you place your expectations in my heart. I have not risen in the morning with anticipation of reading your love letter since I have felt disinterested. I have allowed my circumstances to take control and steal my joy. Thank you for stirring my heart to bring about this change in my emotions, attitude and mind set. I have allowed satan to bring discouragement and have believed his lies. You have showed me the truth of your word today. I give you full control of me and I now make you the Lord of my life. I will tell others of your great love for them and how you set me free from the spirit of deception. In Jesus' Name. Amen.

Refer to the image on page 69 in the book *"Touch Me"*.

Refer to Matthew 16:19 on page 69 in the book *"Touch Me"*.

If you are in a group setting have each person raise their hands for prayer for an unsaved loved one. Let's agree together for their salvation.

Father you have given us the keys to bind and loose. Your word says, "Whatever we bind on earth is bound in heaven and whatever we loose on earth is loosed in heaven." As you called Lazarus forth after being dead for four days . . . we call our loved ones' dry bones to life. We bind the enemy's hold on them and render satan's power ineffective over their soul. We loose the Holy Spirit to take their heart and direct it like a watercourse to Him. We take hold of your promise that everyone in our family will be saved. We bind the spirit of deception and loose the spirit of truth to reign upon them. In Jesus' Name. Amen.

He will give and explain to you a message by means of which you and your entire household (as well) will be saved (from eternal death). (Acts 11:14 AMP)

And they answered, Believe in the Lord Jesus Christ (give yourself up to Him, take yourself out of your own keeping and entrust yourself into His

keeping) and you will be saved, (and this applies both to) you and your household as well. (Acts 16:31 AMP)

Now believe God's word . . . begin to thank Him for their salvation and wait with great expectation for God to show Himself strong in your loved ones!

Read pages 70-71 and refer to the images in the book *"Touch Me"*.

As you read this do you feel the sadness in God's heart?

What is God waiting on you for?

4.   List three things that God's word accomplishes.

Refer to the image on page 71 in the book *"Touch Me"*.

We rescued a little mixed shiatsu named Danny from the SPCA. Some of you have listened to God's Pep Talk that is on our podcast on our blog. (Refer to the back page) All of these messages include Danny and what the Lord has been showing me through this little dog. My husband gives Danny a biscuit and some treats every morning. We watch how he puts them into his mouth and runs into the living room to lay each one of them down. Sometimes he eats a small part of them or saves them for a couple of days. As they have accumulated, I realized he is storing up his treasures.

What treasure are you storing?

Read pages 72-73 in the book *"Touch Me"*.

Answer the four questions in the last paragraph of page 72 in the book *"Touch Me"*.

I used to feel like I was a prisoner in my house and blamed it on my circumstances. However, the Lord showed me that I was imprisoned in my heart. He began to teach me to give my circumstances to Him which freed me from the darkness and enabled me to live in the light of His love. You see, my circumstances hadn't changed yet but I was changing.

As I am finishing this chapter one of my friends sent me an e-mail with the most beautiful and odd streets in the world. As I viewed each one I realized there was an adventure in each one of them. Because of the marking on the first street my eye immediately went to the middle. The second street looked like rolling hills that continued on and on. Another one had tunneled through large trees. The next one looked like the street dropped off into an ocean. One street continued in a circle and it didn't look like you could get anywhere. The next two streets showed them forging through the huge rock formations and the other street was going around them.

Still another street was formed like a race track. Another one was not paved and smooth but looked rough, dirty and dusty. Actually it looked like you would never be able to travel on it. Still another street looked like a roller coaster as it continued up and down and all around. Another street was hidden in all of the foliage and you would wonder how anyone could find that road. Still another one looked like it dropped off the face of the earth since you couldn't see the other side. As I looked at another picture it looked as though it went straight up to the sky. Finally, the last picture was the most serene. The road was right in the middle of beautiful plush greenery that caused you to want to remain there.

I realized these streets represented our journey of life. Sometimes decisions are too hard to make which cause us to straddle the middle of the road. Our emotions play as the stomach churns and we feel that we just can't stay in a situation that continues on and on. Other times we have to tunnel our way through the darkness to see the light. Some situations cause us to check out of life since it's too painful! Sometimes we try to skirt the issues therefore we go around them and never get anything accomplished. Other situations may be so hard that we have to force our way to God in the midst of pain and suffering. Because of the many obligations in this life we feel that we are in a race to accomplish it all. There are times when we are surrounded by tough and hard to deal with people in our lives and tell God, "This assignment is too hard!" There are other times when we feel like we are on a hamster wheel that goes nowhere. Sometimes it seems that no matter what we do life is hard and rough to get through. There are times when we feel we are on a huge roller coaster. One day we are high on the mountain with God and the next we are down in the valley in our emotions. Other times we are wondering where God is hiding and saying, "I don't feel Him anymore." As we listen to all the situations of the world sometimes we are tempted to worry about our future and fear the unknown. Then there are times when we see our prayers touching heaven and we feel like we are in 7th heaven! In the midst of all these times in our journey of life we are on an adventure with God that leads to His love, peace and joy that comes from having an intimate personal relationship with Him!

Will you dare to take this adventure with God and take Him at His word?

Abnormal

Did you ever look at God's creative hand in nature or at someone's gifts, talents or testimony and experience a WOW moment?

But you are a chosen race, a royal priesthood, a dedicated nation; (God's own purchased, special people,(peculiar KJV) that you may set forth the wonderful deeds and display the virtues and perfections of Him Who called you out of darkness into His marvelous light. (I Peter 2:9-10 AMP)

The definition of peculiar is having a character exclusively its own or specific. (Funk and Wagnall)

Think of this . . . . you have been chosen and set apart by God. You are His original design without any duplicates. He has called you out of the darkness of this world into His extraordinary light to display and reveal His excellence and the highest degree of His perfection . . . Not your excellence and perfection.

I can hear most of you saying, "Whoa <u>not</u> WOW!" Many children of God are asking "What is God's plan for me?" Here it is! He has called us to display and reveal His excellence and the highest degree of His perfection to others. I can hear many of you saying, "How can I do that?" After all, that's different from the average person and very abnormal."

Come with me as we walk step by step through the pages of this chapter to a WOW experience!

Read pages 74-76 in the book *"Touch Me"*.

Imagine yourself as a young teen with the whole world ahead of you. You have fallen in love with a man and have been preparing all of your wedding plans with great excitement. You have dreamed about this day since you were a little girl. Now the big day is about to happen. You have never been intimate with him or any other man and have set yourself apart to be intimate with him only after marriage.

However, suddenly all your plans are interrupted. You experience a divine visitation from an angel that informs you that you have been favored by God and have been chosen to carry God's Son. When you don't have the understanding, the angel continues to say that the Holy Spirit will come upon you and the power of God will take control of you. Wow! Talk about a WOW moment! Can you imagine telling your fiancé with whom you have never been intimate? Would he still want to marry you with the thoughts that you have cheated on him? Would your parents believe you? Would you be the latest gossip among the town? Are you in awe of this divine visit or are you concerned about what others will think and say?

Mary asked the angel, "How can it be?" She didn't understand how this would take place at first but when the angel told her the Holy Spirit would come upon her she said, **"Behold, I am the handmaiden of the Lord. Let it be done to me according to what you have said." (Luke 1:38 AMP)**

Refer to the image on page 75 in the book *"Touch Me"*.

Are you looking at what you can't do and not at what God can do or are you giving God all of you so that He can use you in His endless possibilities?

Refer to the first image on page 76 in the book *"Touch Me"*.

Has God handed you a tough assignment?

Mary *believed* the word from God and called herself the hand maiden of the Lord. She *yielded* to God with all of her heart, soul and mind. She *accepted* this assignment over her own plans.

Refer to the second image on page 76 in the book *"Touch Me."*

When God gives you an assignment do you have your running shoes on or have you allowed Him to give you His slippers of rest?

Mary **rested** in the Lord knowing that He had everything under control. She did not allow her emotions to take off with fear, worry and anxiousness of what others would say or how God was going to accomplish His plan and purpose through her. She **trusted** God that He would work everything out according to His plan

So . . . . let's take a look at these steps to a WOW moment!

- Believe that God's word is truth and don't allow doubt in your mind.

Only it must be in faith that he asks with no wavering (no hesitating, no doubting). For the one who wavers (hesitates, doubts) is like the billowing surge out at sea that is blown hither and thither and tossed by the wind. (James 1:6 AMP)

- Yield by giving your emotions and thoughts to the Lord.

Peter started to say to Him, "Behold, we have yielded up and abandoned everything (once and for all and joined you as your disciples, siding with your party) and accompanied you (walking the same road that you walk)." (Mark 10:28 AMP)

- Accept God's plan and agree with His word.

What agreement (can there be between) a temple of God and idols? For we are the temple of the living God; even as God said, "I will dwell in and with and among them and will walk in and with and among them, and I will be their God, and they shall be My people." (II Corinthians 6:16 AMP)

- Rest in the assurance that God has everything under control.

My soul, wait only upon God and silently submit to Him; for my hope and expectation are from Him. (Psalm 62:5 AMP)

- Trust God to work everything out for His purpose and plan.

But I trusted in, relied on, and was confident in You, O Lord; I said, "You are my God." (Psalm 31:14 AMP)

When we are resting and trusting God to work it all out we will be able to hear His voice for our next step. However, when we continually carry the burden while wringing our hands of how and when this will happen and what people will think about us our relationship with God and hearing His voice will be strained.

In Luke 1:36 the angel also tells Mary that her cousin Elizabeth who is way beyond child carrying age and was called barren is in her sixth month of pregnancy. Another WOW moment!

Mary knew the next step was to visit her cousin Elizabeth. Can you see God's plan unfolding to bring confirmation to Mary and take her away from all the negativity!

When God calls us to an assignment He always confirms it and encourages us along the way in the midst of the enemy's negativity.

Read Luke 1:41-42 on page 77 in the book *"Touch Me"*.

Notice Mary didn't defend her divine visitation from the angel. Elizabeth saw the divine favor upon Mary and her baby immediately! Her words confirmed God's word spoken through the angel to Mary.

When I was under a lot of opposition for the ministry, I found myself trying to defend God's spoken word to me. *The Lord spoke to me at that moment. He said, "You do not have to defend my word. My word will be your defense!" I was able to rest in the Lord knowing that He would defend His word. Later I received a phone call from a Pastor that had met me once. The Lord spoke in his heart to call and encourage me that this ministry was of the Lord.*

Are you trying to defend what God has spoken to you to other people?

During this time of separation from Joseph, Mary's parents and other people, God is confirming His word through Elizabeth and the baby within her. This brings much encouragement to Mary in those three months.

Now keep in mind there are no cell phones or any kind of technology for Mary and Joseph to keep in contact. We don't know if she actually told Joseph about the angelic visitation before or after she left for her cousin's home. However, we do know that when she told Joseph he had many thoughts that plagued him.

And her (promised) husband Joseph, being a just and upright man and not willing to expose her publicly and to shame and disgrace her, decided to repudiate and dismiss (divorce) her quietly and secretly. But as he was thinking this over, behold, an angel of the Lord appeared to him in a dream, saying, "Joseph, descendant of David, do not be afraid to take Mary (as) your wife, for that which is conceived in her is of (from, out of) the Holy Spirit."(Matthew 1:19-20 AMP)

Are you beginning to see God's plan unfolding as He has been working behind the scenes?

Imagine yourself sitting in an auditorium watching a drama that portrays your life. There is so much taking place in this journey that you can hardly keep up with it all. You have so many unanswered questions of how, when, what and why! Some things that take place in your life are absolutely breathtaking and other times you feel like you are barely breathing. Then you come to a part of your life that seems like an intermission. Nothing is happening and you have no idea how it will play out! During intermission you usually get up to stretch your legs, get some munchies and whatever else is needed. There is an excitement in the air of how the play will finish. Will it be a happy or sad ending? While you are gone there is much scurrying behind the scenes for all of the props to be set up for the next part of the play. You come back to your seat. The noise has settled down and the curtain opens.

Mary has had three months of intermission. I believe God was building up her spirit to usher in the climax of His plan. Now it's time to return to her fiancé, parents and the towns people.

Can you imagine having to tell Joseph about this baby and hear his reaction while watching the pain of betrayal in his eyes? Yet, she had to trust the Lord that He would work it all out!

Then Joseph, being aroused from his sleep, did as the angel of the Lord had commanded him: he took (her to his side as) his wife. (Matthew 1:24 AMP)

Imagine the ecstasy and anticipation between Mary and Joseph since they both have received a divine visitation about becoming parents of this Holy child! What a WOW experience!

Read Luke 1:13 on pages 77-78 in the book *"Touch Me"*.

Zechariah has been given a WOW moment! But how does he respond?

Read Luke 1:18 on page 78 in the book *"Touch Me"*.

1.   What was the difference between Mary and Zachariah's responses to the divine visitation from God's messenger?

When we compare the Lord's response to Mary and Zachariah we see that Mary had many WOW moments of confirmations and encouragement from the Lord during her nine months of pregnancy. Because of Zachariah's unbelief he was immediately struck with muteness and was not able to talk with Elizabeth and shout his excitement to others! He couldn't thoroughly enjoy those WOW moments until the birth of their son.

What WOW moments have you been given by the Lord? What was your response?

Read page 79 in the book *"Touch Me"*.

Think about the promises that haven't been fulfilled in your life. Are you waiting with a hopeful expectancy and receiving God's encouragement while enjoying His presence or have you given into the enemy's discouragement and no longer seek God for His presence?

If you have given into discouragement are you ready to climb out today?

Seek the Lord and His strength; yearn for and seek His face and to be in His presence continually! (I Chronicles 16:11 AMP)

When we lose something that is valuable to us we search for it immediately and usually don't give up until we retrace all of our steps in our thoughts and actions. So how do we retrace the steps to find God's presence?

- Think about where and when you last felt His presence.

And they who know Your name (who have experience and acquaintance with Your mercy) will lean on and confidently put their trust in You, for You, Lord, have not forsaken those who seek (inquire of and for) You (on the authority of God's Word and the right of their necessity). (Psalm 9:10 AMP)

- What took place in your life that caused you to no longer lean on and place your trust in God's Word?

Then the cares and anxieties of the world and distractions of the age, and the pleasure and delight and false glamour and deceitfulness of riches, and the craving and passionate desire for other things creep in and choke and suffocate the Word, and it becomes fruitless. (Mark 4:19 AMP)

- Did you allow the cares of this world, distractions from the enemy, your own pleasures or passionate desires for other things to choke out the presence of the Lord?

Glory in His holy name; let the hearts of those rejoice who seek and require the Lord (as their indispensable necessity). (Psalm 105:3 AMP)

- When did God stop being the only **One** that could fulfill all of your needs?

Seek, inquire of and for the Lord, and crave Him and His strength (His might and inflexibility to temptation); seek and require His face and His presence (continually) evermore. (Psalm 105:4 AMP)

- When did you stop asking, requiring and desiring His presence that keeps you from temptation continually?

After you have answered these questions honestly . . . . are you ready to get back to your **first love**?

But I have this (one charge to make) against you: that you have left (abandoned) the love that you had at first (you have deserted Me, your first love). Remember then from what heights you have fallen. Repent (change the inner man to meet God's will) and do the works you did previously (when first you knew the Lord), or else I will visit you and remove your lamp stand from its place, unless you change your mind and repent. (Revelations 2:4-5 AMP)

Now that you have retraced your steps to where you lost your **First Love** how do you get back? Are you ready to repent? If so, please pray this with me:

Lord, you have showed me where I lost my First Love. I repent of my negative thinking and behavior towards you and others. I am sorry that I have allowed other people and things (name them all) to take first place in my life. I want to have a greater relationship with you. I *believe* that your word is truth and I ask you to help me not to allow doubt and negativity in my mind. I now *yield* by giving you my emotions and thoughts that brought me discouragement. I *accept* your plan by coming into agreement with Your word. Help me to *rest* in the assurance that You have everything under control and *trust* You to work everything out for Your purpose and plan in my life. In Jesus' Name. Amen.

Now, begin by telling God how much you love Him every day. When you tell Him that you love Him you not only receive a blessing of His presence but you become a blessing to the Lord.

In order to bring about a transformation through God's intervention, He must demolish the destructive behaviors of the past so He can reconstruct your perceptions, thoughts, reasoning, self esteem and so forth that He intended for you.

Step by step as you have interacted with God and others and walked through these chapters, now share what transformation you are beginning to experience physically, emotionally and spiritually?

Read pages 80-81 in the book *"Touch Me"*.

Read Psalm 113:4-6 on page 81 in the book *"Touch Me"*.

One day my daughter called and told me that she had lost a bottle of medicine. She had checked a lot of places that she thought it might be. However, she wasn't able to find it. I said, "When I lose something I ask the Lord where it is since He saw me place it there." We prayed and agreed together that God was going to place a thought in her mind or take her to the place quickly. Within an hour she called me and said, "Mom, you're not going to believe this. I was drying dishes and felt to bend down and open a cupboard door. The medicine was on the shelf." We praised and thanked God together for His faithfulness. That day God conveyed a message to my daughter that she was special to Him!

When you engage God in your everyday life you will begin to see how special you are to Him and how much God loves you!

Read pages 82-83 in the book *"Touch Me"*.

I was experiencing a transformation daily as I continued to spend time in God's presence. Years of pain and sorrow were being washed away as I became more transparent with God and others. I had believed God for a miracle for over twenty years. As my heart and mind were becoming renewed I continued to have great expectation that any day now I would see God's promise. Each day I would look for my miracle like a little child excitedly looking around the corner watching her parents hide gifts under the tree on Christmas Eve. I kept watching for my Daddy's gifts. However, one day I found myself feeling disheartened through toxic thoughts that entered my mind. The waiting period that was leading into discouragement was beginning to overwhelm me. My heart and mind resonated with a sadness that was engulfing me. I began to lose my vitality and felt that every word God had imparted into me was losing grip in my soul. What is even worse is that I felt forsaken by God.

I didn't understand what was happening. He had been teaching and showing me His love in so many ways before this. Surely He didn't stop loving me?

In the midst of the sadness God gave me this vision. I saw myself walking when suddenly I came to a stop. My shoe was sticking to something on the pavement. As I lifted my foot up and looked at my shoe a huge wad of chewing gum was sticking on the bottom of my shoe and the pavement. I believe most of us have stepped into chewing gum at some time or other. My first reaction is "Oh No!" We all have our pet peeves. Well, this is one of mine. I do not appreciate stepping into gum and feel disgusted with the child or thoughtless adult who threw it down. Not only is the bottom of my shoe a mess but I experience my shoe sticking to the floor. As long as the gum remains on my shoe it will begin to pick up other debris such as dirt, paper or candy etc. that has been dropped. If I have smashed it down into my shoe it is even harder to remove so I usually have to find some kind of instrument to help pry it loose.

God began to show me that I was stuck between discouragement and hope. I had allowed the toxic thoughts to take control of my mind and emotions. God had given me His spoken and written words, visions and dreams for this miracle throughout the years that was building my faith and advancing me into God's kingdom while teaching it out to others. But I was stuck in sadness and despair and couldn't seem to climb out of the misery that I felt. I couldn't move forward in the calling that God had for me and felt disabled. I needed an intervention of God's instrument of hope to release me from this transfixion in my heart and mind.

The following day in the midst of the sadness in my soul a song rose up in my spirit. "All things are possible!" One line says, "There's nothing He can't do when you expect Him to!" I began to feel His spirit taking control of my flesh. God had come to my rescue! Suddenly I felt the Holy Spirit taking my flesh quickly through this dark chamber hollowing out the wall of sadness while leading me into His light!

I realized that satan had showed up with toxic thoughts that had stolen my expectations that led me into a darkened chamber beneath my emotions and caused me to fall into his trap of discouragement.

81

Jenny Hagemeyer

Sometimes our life feels like this chewing gum sticking to our shoes. When we lift our shoe we can't pull away since it's still stuck to the pavement. Trials come along that bring despair and we become stuck between discouragement and hope. It becomes an effort to continue reading God's word and praying.

We begin to pick up the debris of fear, worry and anxiousness that walk with discouragement. We become entrenched in the sadness that stops us from advancing in our life. But . . . Child of God, don't lose heart . . . suddenly God shows up! He has not forsaken you and is hovering over you right now. He has come to your rescue.

Be strong and let your heart take courage, all you who wait for and hope for and expect the Lord! (Psalm 31:24 AMP)

Are you stuck between discouragement and hope? If you are in a group setting the leader should pray this. If you are not in a group setting pray this prayer for yourself.

Holy Spirit, I ask that you rescue each person (me) today that has been stuck between discouragement and hope. I ask that your presence engulf them (me). Let them (me) feel you taking hold of their (my) hand leading them (me) out of this darkness. Thank you. Your deliverance has led them (me) back to placing their (my) hope in you. In Jesus Name. Amen.

So . . . I am going to ask you to envision Jesus taking your hand while holding an instrument marked HOPE. Can you see Him? He says to you, "My child, I have come to rescue you. Don't let go." You begin walking together through the narrow corridors of pain and sorrow when you come upon a wall. You wonder how Jesus can take you through this. Jesus takes His instrument of Hope and begins hollowing out a darkened wall of sadness. You continue to hold on while climbing up with Him as the hole becomes larger. He begins to sing a song that says, "All things are possible. There's nothing I can't do when you expect Me too." He looks at you and says, "My Child, do you expect me to bring you out of this?" Your answer is "Yes!" Suddenly the wall disappears. He takes His instrument of Hope and hands it to you. He says, "It is done!" Suddenly you are out of the darkened chamber of sadness and are filled with His hope, love and joy. Jesus has rescued you! Now receive your breakthrough in Jesus' Name! He has led you to the light of His deliverance! Lift up your voice of praise!

You, who bring good tidings to Zion, go up on a high mountain. You who bring good tidings to Jerusalem, lift up your voice with a shout. Lift it up, do not be afraid; say to the towns of Judah, "Here is your God!" (Isaiah 40:9 NIV)

Refer to image on page 83 in the book *"Touch Me"*.

Do you see God as small as a red bird and your circumstances as large as a tree or your circumstances as small as the red bird and your God larger than a tree?

Read pages 84-85 in the book *"Touch Me"*.

As I kept seeking the Lord for His divine wisdom I received a phone call from a friend of mine. She told me to check the information on the internet on shingles. Notice I was walking down the steps to my computer when God spoke to me. He directed my steps away from the computer and towards His spoken and written word to me.

In all your ways know, recognize, and acknowledge Him, and He will direct and make straight and plain your paths. (Proverbs 3:6 AMP)

When I heard God's still small voice in my spirit I felt His love surround me and was enveloped in His peace and joy. God's encouraging words took precedence over discouragement from the enemy and brought me hope. As I continued to speak His healing word my spirit began to rise above the negativity of my flesh. Now, I am not saying it would have been bad for me to check out the computer. I am saying that as I was asking God for His divine direction and wisdom He directed me away from the computer.

I had another situation when my mother was having severe cramps in her body. As we prayed together I felt to check out some natural remedies on the computer. I was able to find a natural product that relieved the pain from the cramps within seconds. We knew that was an answer to prayer along with speaking God's word of healing for my mother.

May all those who seek, inquire of and for You, and require You (as their vital need) rejoice and be glad in You; and may those who love Your salvation say continually, "Let God be magnified!" (Psalm 70:4 AMP)

When a problem arises in our life we must place our focus on God who is the solution and has the answer! When we magnify God we will no longer magnify the problem.

When you experience an illness do you magnify Jehovah Rophe (Healer) in the sickness or do you magnify the negativity of the sickness?

Refer to the image on page 85 in the book *"Touch Me"*.

I'm going to ask you to place instrumental music on. If you are in a group setting have the leader read this. If you are not in a group setting, place instrumental music on while speaking this for yourself.

Now close your eyes and imagine yourself at the bottom of a mountain. As you look up Jesus is standing at the top waiting for you to come to Him. You want to join Him but find that every step is a great effort. You say, "Jesus the path is too hard and I am tired." He says, "My child look at what you are carrying? You have a back pack on with burdens that I have not given you to carry. Take your back pack off and let me show you the burdens." (Ask Jesus to reveal the burdens you are carrying) Now take your back pack off and begin to give those burdens to Jesus. Now that you have given those burdens . . . . RUN to meet Jesus! He has been waiting for you!

I encourage you to continue this exercise in your quiet time with the Lord. If you are praying and listening to a lot of problems from others you may have picked up their burdens along with yours that you may not be aware of.

I'd like to share a time when I was not aware of carrying this burden. Recently I was invited to sing in two churches on a Sunday morning. For days my focus was on the continued questions in my mind surrounding this experience. During this time I was sitting outside on our back yard talking to the Lord. I heard Him ever so gently say in my spirit, "I didn't give this opportunity to burden you. I gave this to you so I could show myself strong through you." I could feel His love and concern for me. Immediately I asked Him to forgive me and thanked Him for this opportunity. His joy began to rise up within me and I began to look forward to His open door of opportunity!

When I made this assignment about me it became a burden. When I saw this as God's open door of opportunity it was no longer about me but God showing Himself strong through me.

Perhaps you have been given an open door of opportunity from God. Are you making this assignment about you or about God showing Himself strong through you?

Refer to the image on page 86 in the book ***"Touch Me"***.

Maybe you have a situation going on in your life right now. You've been wondering why, how or when? Here is your answer. "GOD KNOWS WHY, HOW AND WHEN!" And . . . when you seek Him with all your heart He will show you in His timing!

And Jehoshaphat said to the king of Israel, Inquire first, I pray you, for the word of the Lord today. (II Chronicles 18:4 AMP)

Refer to image on page 87 in the book ***"Touch Me"***.

When I took the wrong path notice I made it much harder for myself. Sometimes I've heard other people justify taking the wrong path by saying, "I'm not hurting anyone else." So . . . let me ask you this question. How do you feel when you see your children taking the wrong path? When my daughter was on the wrong path I remember talking with her on the phone while weeping because of the pain that I felt for her. I only wanted the best for her. I believe that God weeps for us when we decide to go our own way or are led by other people's expectations.

How can I give you up, Ephraim? How can I hand you over, Israel? How can I treat you like Admah? How can I make you like Zeboiim? My heart is changed within me; all my compassion is aroused. (Hosea 11:8 NIV)

God loved His children in the midst of their disobedience. He knew the consequences of sin and His heart was breaking for them.

Can you hear the compassion God had for His children? Can you feel His heart breaking? Ask God to break your heart for what breaks His.

Recently I was scheduled for a book signing in a Christian Bookstore. I met a woman who loved the Lord with all of her heart. She had a daughter that was on the wrong path. As she relayed the events to me while crying, I heard the compassion and love in her tender heart towards her daughter.

I was able to identify with the pain in her heart and also to give her encouragement in the midst of sorrow. I shared with her a dream that God gave me one night that gave me tremendous peace. Even though I knew that God loved my daughter more than I ever could I was tormented by fearful thoughts of the dangers of what if and if only!

As I continued to cry out for her I had this dream. I saw my daughter slipping down further into a deep well. There was no effort on her part to climb out. Every move took her down until she finally reached the bottom of the well. However, when she hit bottom there was no where to look except up! At the top of the well I saw Jesus with His arms reaching down to pull her out. I felt His compassion as I saw Jesus reach down first and then she took hold of His hand. As I was writing this I pictured how it would be if she was a little child and had fallen into the well because she disobeyed her daddy. How would her daddy react when he saw his little girl down at the bottom of a well? A loving father would reach down with his strong arms and tell her to take his hand. I believe that He would say, "It's going to be okay. Don't be afraid. Now, Honey you must listen and do what I tell you too. Daddy is here and he will help you out of this. Take hold of my hand and I will lift you up!"

Maybe you have a child that is on the wrong path and you have been crying out for them for many years. God wants you to hear His heart for your child. He has not forgotten or forsaken your child. He loves them more than you could ever love them.

There is a song that says, "There is none like you. No one else can touch my heart like you do." Another part of this says, "Suffering children are safe in your arms."

When God gave me this dream, I was surrounded by His peace that enabled me to give Him my daughter. I prayed Psalm 91 and personalized it with my daughter's name. If you have been trying to change your child and have not succeeded perhaps you have never placed them in Jesus' arms! As long as you continue to try to change them they will stay in rebellion. When I asked the Lord to change my heart towards her I began to see changes in her.

When you show them who you are in the Lord they will begin to see who they can be with the Lord.

Maybe **you** are the little child that wondered off the path from God and have fallen into a deep well. Your Daddy God is reaching down to you. He is not angry at you. He loves you with an everlasting love. He has not left or forsaken you. He has been waiting for you to look up to Him and see his hand. Won't you take His hand now?

A Shepherd never drives the sheep He always leads them.

Are you on a path led by God's instructions or a path driven by your will or other people's expectations? Take this time to ask the Lord. He will show you if you are being driven or led.

Read pages 88-90 in the book *"Touch Me"*.

Sometimes we carry the burdens knowingly and other times we have no idea what is going on inside of us.

I had a very hurtful situation that caught me off guard and actually placed me into a panic in my emotions. One night while I was sleeping the Lord spoke this into my spirit. "I am bringing these weaknesses out in you so I can perfect them."

But he said to me, "My grace is sufficient for you, for my power is made perfect in weakness. Therefore I will boast all the more gladly about my

weaknesses, so that Christ's power may rest on me." (II Corinthians 12:9 NIV)

The Amplified Bible says it like this: But He said to me, "My grace (My favor and loving-kindness and mercy) is enough for you (sufficient against any danger and enables you to bear the trouble manfully); for My strength and power are made perfect (fulfilled and completed) and show themselves most effective in (your) weakness." Therefore, I will all the more gladly glory in my weaknesses and infirmities, that the strength and power of Christ (the Messiah) may rest (yes, may pitch a tent over and dwell) upon me!

Did you catch this? Because of Jesus' death and resurrection His strength and power pitches a tent over you and dwells upon you.

The following night I woke up at 2:00 A.M. weeping uncontrollably. Afterwards, I felt peace in my spirit and knew that God was healing me. However, two days later my emotions got out of hand and I was back in a panic. For months I had negativity in my mind on what some other people thought about me. The words were spoken over me through another person and I had taken them into my heart and mind. Let me convey something about myself. "I do not and have never liked confrontations." However, I had been praying all those months whether to confront or not. God knew what it took for me to see that He wanted to end this grievous pain within me. I kept hearing these words in my spirit. "Enough is enough!"

He literally pitched a tent by setting up camp over my heart and mind and resided over my emotions until I confronted this issue. I was entrenched in these emotional wounds. It was time to find out if this was a lie in my mind or truth in their heart. God showed me the truth that confiscated the lies of the enemy in my heart and mind.

I believe when we do our part God will do His part.

Even though I do not feel comfortable with confrontations notice I was praying for God's wisdom on whether or not to confront it. One morning our Pastor Steve Watkins had a message on confronting your fears. I knew in my heart that God was saying it was time but I didn't have the courage to confront the fear of rejection until God faced me with this emotional wound that I was carrying for many years. As long as the lies remained in my mind I wasn't able to hear the truth that would bring reconciliation. You see I thought as long as it wasn't affecting me emotionally I didn't need to confront it and God would deal with it. God knew that I wouldn't be able to let this burden go until He faced me with it.

Perhaps you need to confront an issue in your life that you have been carrying for many months or perhaps even years. If so, please pray this with me.

Father, show me whether I am waiting on you to resolve this issue or you are waiting on me to confront this in your love. Your word says that fear is torment. I bind the spirit of torment and thank you for a sound mind. I ask that you show me whether or not this is a lie in my mind or truth in their heart. I bind the spirit of fear that is keeping me from not accepting what you say about me. I choose to do your will and trust that you will give me your timing, words of wisdom and guidance. I ask that you open my mouth and fill it with your words.

Thank you for preparing their heart to receive the words from your Holy Spirit in order to bring reconciliation. In Jesus' Name. Amen.

If God shows you not to confront at this time or maybe never . . . continue on His path of doing right and in God's appointed season you will reap the harvest of His revealing truth.

And let us not lose heart and grow weary and faint in acting nobly and doing right, for in due time and at the appointed season we shall reap, if we do not loosen and relax our courage and faint. (Galatians 6:9 AMP)

Read pages 90-92 in the book *"Touch Me"*.

Refer to the image on page 92 in the book *"Touch Me"*.

So . . . let's talk about what it means to lay your Isaac's on the altar.

At the age of seventy five Abraham received his calling to leave his country and follow God's leading to another country with a promise from God.

Now, (In Heran) the Lord said to Abram, "Go for yourself (for your own advantage) away from your country, from your relatives and your father's house, to the land that I will show you.

And I will make of you a great nation, and I will bless you (with abundant increase of favors) and make your name famous and distinguished, and you will be a blessing (dispensing good to others)." (Genesis 12:1-2 AMP)

So . . . Abram pulled up stakes and left his country with many of his relatives and friends left behind. The Bible doesn't talk about the emotions or thoughts of Abram in hearing this word from God. However, I believe that even though his thoughts and emotions are not recorded like David's in the book of Psalms he had to lay down **his own understanding** and the **fear of the unknown** on God's altar of sacrifice in order to trust God's plan for his life. Abram was embarking on the journey of life trusting the Lord no matter where God would lead him.

When God called me to another county I had no idea that it would be a long term commitment. For seven years my thoughts were, "I don't want to be here and I can't wait to go back. How long, Lord, how long?" One day a lady prayed for me at a meeting and told me that God called me here.

I was so upset that I cried until there were no tears left. I said, "God, I don't want to be called here but if you have called me change my heart!" When I came to the end of my emotions Jesus took hold of them and changed my heart two weeks later!

Perhaps you have been called to pull up stakes and move to another county or state or even out of the country? What was your reaction?

Read Genesis 12:7-10

After traveling over eight hundred miles, God appears to Abram in the land of Canaan telling him that this is where He is calling him to settle. At that time the land was in a famine and the Canaanites were morally corrupt. God led Abraham to continue on to Egypt and remain there until the famine ended. Think about how you would feel traveling all those miles for many days or perhaps even months? Can you imagine traveling on those dry and dusty desert trails not knowing where your destination would be? Even today with our luxurious travel I begin to get anxious and ready to arrive at our destination. It's great when I am no longer cooped up in a car and am able to stretch my legs and walk. Think about the anticipation of living in another country and adjusting to a whole new life. How had he envisioned the new land to be? Why did God call him to leave the land of good and plenty and journey to a God forsaken land full of corruptness, perversion and famine? After all, God had a great plan to bless him and others through him. Abram had to lay down **his expectations** on God's altar of sacrifice and allow God to place His expectations within him. He had to lay down **his disappointments** and allow God to give His appointment.

As Abram continues to be obedient to God's word God comes to him the third time but this time in a vision saying, **"Fear not, Abram, I am your Shield, your abundant compensation, and your reward shall be exceedingly great." (Genesis 15:1-2 AMP)**

Abram begins to ask God about having an heir to his household since he and Sarah have continued to be childless. God gives him the following promise of being the father of many nations. So a dialogue takes place between Abram and God as Abram asks the questions and God answers him.

And Abram said, "Lord God, what can you give me, since I am going on (from this world) childless and he who shall be the owner and heir of my house is this (steward) Eliezer of Damascus? And Abram continued, Look, You have given me no child; and (a servant) born in my house is my heir." And behold, the word of the Lord came to him, saying, "This man shall not be your heir, but he who shall come from your own body shall be your heir. And He brought him outside (his tent into the starlight) and said, look now toward the heavens and count the stars if you are able to number them. Then He said to him, so shall your descendants be." (Genesis 15:2-5 AMP)

And he (Abram) believed in (trusted in, relied on, remained steadfast to) the Lord, and He counted it to him as righteousness (right standing with God). (Genesis 15:6 AMP)

Here is where we can hear the heart of Abram. Can you hear some discouragement as the years are moving on and still the promise of God has not been fulfilled? As God brought encouragement to Abram through His word he had to lay down the **temptation to waver in his thoughts of having an heir** and remain committed with unwavering faith in God's promise of an heir.

Read Genesis 16:1-16

However, in the waiting period while laying these sacrifices on the altar Sarah convinced Abram to have a child with her Egyptian servant, Hagar. For many years Abraham and Sarai prayed for a son. It had been ten years of unanswered prayers. In a moment of weakness Sarai came up with a plan of having a son. She took the plan to Abram and he succumbed to her plan instead of waiting for God's plan. Notice in verse two Abram listened to the voice of his wife instead of the voice of God. Abram needed to lay down **Sarai's plan** on the altar of God's sacrifice and hold onto God's plan.

And Sarai said unto Abram, "Behold now, the Lord hath restrained me from bearing: I pray thee, go in unto my maid; it may be that I may obtain children by her." And Abram hearkened to the voice of Sarai. (Genesis 16:2 KJ)

Instead of resting in the promises of God they tried to help God accomplish the fulfillment of His promises. Out of this union between eighty six year old Abram and Hagar, a son whom God called Ishmael, which means the Lord hears, was born.

How many times have you given up on the promises of God and tried to help fulfill His promise with your plan?

Read and meditate on Genesis 17:1-22

Abram was ninety-nine years old when God came to him the fourth time after he arrived in the land of Canaan. God promised to establish an everlasting covenant with Abram and all of his descendants if Abram walked blameless before Him and displayed integrity. This time there is no dialogue between Abram and God. Abram fell with his face down in awe of God while God continued to speak. In this Abrahamic covenant God promised the land of Canaan as an everlasting possession but commanded that all male babies must be circumcised which represented a thorough commitment to God. On that very day Abram obeyed God and called the males together for circumcision along with himself and Ishmael. Now we see a significant step in Abram's life as he receives a promotion from God. God no longer calls him Abram (Exalted Father) but gives him the name Abraham which means Father of Many. His wife Sarai receives the name Sarah along with all of the promised blessings given to Abraham. At this time in his life he has believed and trusted God's promises for twenty four years. Not only has God established this covenant but He also sets a time of one year for the birth of Isaac. How did Abraham react to this? He fell on his face and laughed since he and Sarah were way past birthing years. Had he given up on the promise of Sarai's conception since they were not able to conceive in their younger years? Had he thought about his father, Terah who had lived to be two hundred and five years old which showed that he could have a much longer life expectancy? In order to believe the promise from God, Abraham had to lay down **his timing** on God's altar of sacrifice and allow God to give His timing.

Read Genesis 18:1-19

A pivotal event occurs when three men visit Abraham and Sarah. One believed to be the Lord with two angels at his side.

For the first time in all these years of God's promises to Abraham, Sarah hears the word of the Lord's promise of a son and laughs. How could this be possible since she is way past childbearing years? After all she didn't know anyone that had a child at her age. I thought about why the Lord and two angels came. The number three in the Bible represents resurrection and divine completion. I believe God was not only confirming His promise to Sarah but was bringing the divine completion of their prayers for many years. God was resurrecting hope for the promise of a son. The Lord asked, "Abraham, is anything too hard or too wonderful for the Lord?" An appointed season was coming and they were to wait with great expectation for the Lord to open Sarah's womb to bring about the birth of Isaac. They had to lay down their **old mindsets** on God's altar of sacrifice and allow God to change their thoughts to connect with His heart.

Perhaps you have lost hope for God's promise. If so, ask God to reveal your old mindsets so you can lay them down on God's altar. This allows God to change your thoughts, connect with His heart and resurrect hope within you.

Read Genesis 21:1-8

Finally after all the promises from God for an heir, Abraham and Sarah conceive a long awaited son whom God names Isaac, which means laughter. Can you imagine after all these years of the pain of being barren the promise of a son has been fulfilled? Praise God! He has worked a miracle in their life. Now is the time for a celebration! God has proved that nothing is impossible for Him. Love resonates in their spirit, joy is resurrected in their hearts and the pain of the past is healed as they laugh and experience the newness of life with their baby boy. Each day is exciting as they watch Isaac discovering new things about himself and others.

Read Genesis 22:1-19

Then one day God reveals Himself to Abraham for the seventh time with a test of proving his love for God. Did he love God more than his son or his son more than God? God and Abraham had developed a close relationship of trusting each other. In the beginning God spoke and Abraham listened and obeyed. Later God came to him in a vision that brought a conversation between them.

Abraham asked God questions and was honest with his feelings. When Abraham needed proof of what God would do God reminded him of what he had done in the past and how He protected him. Every time God visited Abraham He brought encouragement for the future and many promised blessings. After all he was even visited by the Lord with two angels at his side. He had entertained the Lord in his home and served him food and drink for nourishment. Abraham had learned how to lay his mind, will and emotions on the altar of God's sacrifice. What would he lay down now? Isaac was the long awaited miracle from God. We don't know exactly how old Isaac was but in verse 6 Abraham placed the wood for the burnt offering on Isaac. Therefore, some believe he could have been 10-16 years old. Was God revealing Abraham's character? Would he trust God enough to still believe in the promises? Was his son more precious than his relationship with God? After all, Abraham was called a friend of God.

And (so) the Scripture was fulfilled that says, Abraham believed in (adhered to, trusted in, and relied on) God, and this was accounted to him as righteousness (as conformity to God's will in thought and deed), and he was called God's friend. (James 2:23 AMP)

You are My friends if you keep on doing the things which I command you to do. I do not call you servants (slaves) any longer, for the servant does not know what his master is doing (working out). But I have called you My friends, because I have made known to you everything that I have heard from My Father. (I have revealed to you everything that I have learned from Him.) (John 15:14-15 AMP)

God called Abraham a friend because he did everything God commanded him to. Therefore, God trusted Abraham to let him know the future. I believe that Abraham saw God as his friend also and learned that he could trust and rely on God's word. Therefore, in laying down his human weaknesses he allowed God to perfect those weaknesses in him. Abraham showed his complete trust in God when it came to this test of love and proved that he loved God more than his son.

So what do we have to do in order to obey God in laying our Isaac's on the altar?

1. Lay down our understanding.

2. Lay down the fear of the unknown.

3. Lay down our expectations.

4. Lay down our disappointments.

5. Lay down the temptation to waver in our thoughts.

6. Lay down the plans of others and our own.

7.　　Lay down our timing.

8.　　Lay down our old mindsets.

Who or what is your Isaac? Have you taken these steps to lay down your Isaac and experience God's love? Abraham was given the ultimate test of love. Did he love Isaac more or less than God?

If anyone comes to Me and does not hate his (own) father and mother (in the sense of indifference to or relative disregard for them in comparison with his attitude toward God) and (likewise) his wife and children and brothers and sisters—(yes) and even his own life also—he cannot be My disciple. (Luke 14:26 AMP)

This scripture is not meaning hate as we view hate in this world. The Greek word for hate means to love less. (Strong's)

Read pages 93-94 in the book, *"Touch Me"*.

Refer to the image on page 93 in the book, *"Touch Me"*.

Perhaps you have laid your Isaac on God's altar of sacrifice and have snatched your loved one or situation back. In the midst of taking these steps in trusting God I still experienced a deep grief. However, God was faithful in the midst of the pain and suffering and showed me the deep dark tunnel that I was in. The Holy Spirit brought me comfort in the midst of my discomfort. Even though I didn't understand God's timing for my brother's death He gave me the gift of understanding other's deep grief.

The other day I was changing a clock in our car that was set at a certain time. Every time I tried to change the time it would go back to the set time. Try as I might I could not get the steps to the process in the right order until I got the manual out and read it. I had to follow the step by step process in order to make the change. God has a step by step process in your journey of life with Him. He has written a manual, which is His word, for you to read every day for instruction and direction in your life. When you asked Jesus into your heart, the Holy Spirit came to guide you into all truth and comfort and counsel you no matter what you are going through.

This has been the longest exercise in this guide. When I was writing this I kept trying to move ahead. The Holy Spirit spoke in my spirit not to miss a step. I believe that this exercise is **vitally important** to have God's freedom in your mind and heart in order to experience the abundant life on this earth. Ask God what steps you have not taken in order to experience His freedom in whatever situation you are in.

So . . . the question is, "Is God first place in your life?" Do you love Him more or less than your life or your loved ones? If you are in a group setting or by yourself take this time to review the steps and ask the Holy Spirit to show you what steps you have not taken to lay your Isaac on God's altar of sacrifice and pray this with me.

Father, forgive me for placing my Isaacs before you. Holy Spirit, reveal what steps I have missed in being able to lay my Isaac's on your altar of sacrifice. In this time of unanswered prayers help me to rest in your promises and not to try to help you accomplish the fulfillment of your promise. Help me not to love my life and loved ones more than you. Help me to be obedient to your word in Jesus Name. Amen.

Read page 95 in the book, *"Touch Me"*.

2.   What is the definition of reject?

Notice the dialogue that took place between the Holy Spirit and me.

- I did not realize that I had a fear of being rejected by others until I cried out to God and said, "Why am I crying all the time after these meetings?" God said, "You are afraid of being rejected."
- God allowed another painful rejection in my life to shine His light on the darkness of rejection which brought me to cry out and say, "Why are you allowing this rejection?" God said, "I'm using this to heal you of rejection.

It was hard for me to imagine that this painful incident in my life was going to bring healing and free me from this rejection.

However, this incident gave me even more reason to cry out to God for freedom from rejection. The Holy Spirit spoke in my heart that I had a root to the rejection. He told me the root was my birth father.

Read pages 96-97 in the book ***"Touch Me"***.

So what is a root? In a plant it is defined as an underground base of the plant that anchors and absorbs water and nutrients from the soil. The root is embedded, fixed and immobile until you pull the root out of the ground. Therefore, the root is the source for which the plant derives its life.

I believe the day I was told about my birth father at twelve years old a root of rejection began. Throughout the years the negative thoughts on what was wrong with me continued to grow as I experienced more rejection from others. The root of rejection in my heart was being fed the nutrients of satan's lies which allowed the root to stay embedded in my heart and fixed in my mind. It remained immobile for all those years until God revealed the root and began a healing process many years later!

As long as we live in a fallen world of imperfection rejection is inevitable. If you haven't experienced rejection yet . . . you will. Our human nature desires for everyone to accept us. We have an innate longing to be loved. Yet the only one who will ever love you with perfect unconditional love is God!

There are different types of rejection.

- Self-rejection

- Rejection from others

- Projection of rejection

As I was writing this section of the study guide, I received a phone call from one of the ladies on our team. While choking back the tears, she began to relay an incident that had taken place. Frustration had soared to an all time high in her emotions that caused her to feel there was something dreadfully wrong with her. Satan had placed her head on his chopping block and was dishing out dreadful punishment in her mind for her reactions. My heart connected with her pain as she revealed more of the anger that she felt towards herself. She told me that for weeks she had been so frustrated when she had to change a pooped diaper. She couldn't understand why she was so upset every time this situation occurred. After all, it didn't bother her before. However, today was the worst of it. One of the children had a blow out that splattered on her new carpet. Worst of all, the little child stepped into it and smeared it in all different spots. In her frustration she let loose of the anger on her husband and her children. Now, please don't misunderstand how I am conveying this message.

There was no abuse and afterwards, she apologized for her behavior towards them. The problem was that she couldn't forgive herself. Satan welcomed this situation to beat her up with his accusing thoughts. In the years that I have known her this delightful young woman has been wounded with self rejection. I tried to picture how I would feel with this incident and I couldn't see myself being very gracious either without engaging the Holy Spirit to help me. C'mon you know what I am talking about!

As we prayed and sought the Lord's healing in her mind and emotions, I realized that satan was feeding her mind with toxic thoughts that I will refer to as **SATAN'S POOP**! I can hear some of you laughing right now wondering why in the world I placed this into the guide.

The definition for poop is the unproductive, undigested waste material that must be refused and pushed out of place to keep us healthy. (Funk and Wagnall)

I began to think about an acronym for each letter of the word POOP!

Protrusive . . . means pushing or driving forward.

Obtrusive . . . means to force or thrust an opinion.

Oppressive . . . means burdensome, tyrannical, harsh and cruel.

Plot . . . means to plan for secretly, a secret plan to accomplish some questionable purpose; conspiracy. (Funk and Wagnall)

So . . . we can say, "Satan pushes his thoughts forward in our mind to force his opinions about ourselves/others that are burdensome, harsh, tyrannical and cruel. He schemes while secretly waiting for the right situation or moment to accomplish conspiracy against God and His creation."

The spirit of rejection blocks you from receiving the truth of God's word.

Read and meditate on Ephesians 1:4-5 on page 97-98 in the book **"Touch Me".**

When you adopt a child you choose to have them in your family and treat them as though you were the birth parents. Therefore, everything you own is theirs.

The Greek meaning for the word adopted is Sonship. (Strong's)

For (the Spirit which) you have now received (is) not a spirit of slavery to put you once more in bondage to fear, but you have received the Spirit of adoption (the Spirit producing sonship) in (the bliss of) which we cry, Abba (Father)! Father! (Romans 8:15 AMP)

Refer to the image on page 98 in the book **"Touch Me".**

The spirit of rejection blocks you from receiving God's love.

- Jesus **chose** to give His life for you.

- Jesus **took** all of our punishment on the cross so we would receive God's grace . . . not what we deserve.

- Jesus **volunteered** to be the donor of His precious blood for you in order to start the flow of God's love.

Can you picture this scene in your mind? Think about how you would react towards someone who **chose** to save your life and died so you could live?

For God so greatly loved and dearly prized the world that He (even) gave up His only begotten (unique) Son, so that whoever believes in (trusts in,

clings to, relies on) Him shall not perish (come to destruction, be lost) but have eternal (everlasting) life. For God did not send the Son into the world in order to judge (to reject, to condemn, to pass sentence on) the world, but that the world might find salvation and be made safe and sound through Him. (John 3:16-17 AMP)

When you truly grasp the love God has for you it will completely change your life.

Read page 99-100 in the book ***"Touch Me"***.

When we have been rejected and continue to carry hidden pain what takes place in our mind and heart?

Are you projecting rejection with an expectation of being rejected? If so, have you asked the Lord to reveal the rejection and remove the hidden pain?

Some of you may not be aware of a root to rejection so I would like to ask you to pray this with me:

Father, many painful situations have taken place in my life that I have not understood. Other people have rejected me that have caused me to reject myself and feel unworthy of your love. I ask for your divine revelation for healing in my heart and reveal the root of my insecurities. Your word says that I am not to lean on my own understanding but in all my ways you will direct my path. Thank you for showing me the root to this rejection. In Jesus Name. Amen.

When we accept rejection we:

- Disagree with who God says we are.

- Place man's acceptance as more important than God's.

- Believe the lies of the enemy.

Refer to the image on page 100 in the book ***"Touch Me"***.

The definition of define is to give form or meaning to. (Funk and Wagnall)

Are not two little sparrows sold for a penny? And yet not one of them will fall to the ground without your Father's leave (consent) and notice. But even the very hairs of your head are all numbered. Fear not, then; you are of more value than many sparrows. (Matthew 10:29-31 AMP)

Do you receive your value from God or do you look to your job, spouse, business, fame, wealth or other people for your worth?

One day I was talking with one of the ladies on our team. She was having a very difficult time in her emotions. Satan's harsh and cruel words about herself were piercing her mind. As I was praying with her I received a vision. I saw Jesus with a gavel in His hand. He took the gavel and hit it on a stand. He said, "I'll be the judge of that!" When this precious woman listened to the enemy's words she was not able to receive God's word of His acceptance and love for her. She could not see that she was God's handiwork and that He was crafting her by His hand to do His work. As a result she felt that she didn't and couldn't measure up to her expectations or to the expectation of others.

As long as you try to measure up to your own and to other people's expectations you will never be able to receive God's acceptance. When you receive God's acceptance you will be able to accept yourself.

Refer to images on page 101 in the book *"Touch Me"*.

God showed me that I couldn't reflect His light as long as I allowed the spirit of rejection to steal God's glory and splendor from my heart and mind. As God began to reveal the root of rejection it enabled me to give the pain to Him. He began to polish and refine those dull areas within my heart in order to see His reflection within me.

For we are God's (own) handiwork (His workmanship), recreated in Christ Jesus, (born anew) that we may do those good works which God predestined (planned beforehand) for us (taking paths which He prepared ahead of time), that we should walk in them (living the good life which He prearranged and made ready for us to live). (Ephesians 2:10 AMP)

When you receive God's acceptance of your weaknesses

- Self hatred dissipates;

- The spirit of torment departs;

- You receive God's perspective of you and other people;

- God's light shines in your heart;

- Your life is no longer about your plan but His plan;

- You fall into His arms of acceptance;

- You eagerly receive God's word daily;

- You no longer criticize other people to make yourself look better;

- You see that God's grace is sufficient. (II Corinthians 12:9)

So . . . here are three questions:

1. Were you wounded or rejected by a spouse, parent, close friend or family member? What was your reaction?
2. If so, have you chosen to forgive them and allow God to change your heart towards them or are you still carrying the wound?
3. If you are still carrying wounds are you ready for God to reveal the root of rejection?

Let's outline what we have discussed so far.

- The definition of reject is cast away, worthless, discard, to refuse to accept or recognize.

- There are three types . . . self-rejection, rejection from others, projection of rejection.

- Illustration of self rejection.

- Satan's poop.

- Spirit of rejection blocks truth of God's word and receiving God's love.

- We will project the rejection on others if hidden pain isn't removed.

- Prayer for God's revelation of the root of rejection.

- What happens when you accept rejection?

- God defines you.

- Receiving God's acceptance.

Now that you have received enlightenment of God's word about His love and acceptance let's talk about how to get rid of the enemy of rejection.

Read pages 102-104 in the book *"Touch Me"*.

Read and Meditate on Hebrews 12:1, Matthew 3:10 and Proverbs 8:19.

Refer to image on page 103 in the book *"Touch Me"*.

So you must choose to throw off everything that hinders your relationship with God and repent of the sin of rejection and justification that has entangled you. When you refuse the worthless rubbish in your heart, God takes His axe and cuts out the deadness in your heart that has prevented you from accepting the truth of His word and receiving God's love. He takes the dead wood of satan's accusations and throws it into His incinerator and burns it up with His love, compassion, mercy and grace. The fruit of God's spirit becomes evident in your walk with Him and others see and experience the love of Jesus within you. When the rejection comes knocking at your door the Holy Spirit will help you to recognize the spirit of rejection and tell you not to answer it. **Refuse the refuse!**

If you have been abandoned or experienced abuse by your earthly father please hear your Heavenly Father's heart for you. Before you begin this exercise pray this with me.

Father, I ask you to open up my heart so I can hear your heart for me. I ask you to send your healing power for my heart and mind. I give you every painful word that has been spoken over me or about me. Thank you for removing the hidden pain that has caused me to feel worthless and unaccepted. I receive your acceptance and believe every word that you say about me. Thank you for choosing me to be your Child. In Jesus' Name. Amen.

This is a time for the Holy Spirit to bring healing. Some of you have been so wounded that you have not been able to receive God's love. I am going to ask you to place instrumental music on. Imagine your loving Heavenly Father having this conversation with you. I'm going to ask the leader of your group to speak these sentences slowly. If you are not in a group please speak them slowly to yourself. Please take your time to allow the Holy Spirit to work His healing in your heart.

- I am your Father.

- I picked you out for Myself to be my child.

- I will never abuse or abandon you.

- You are precious in My sight.

- I have been calling out your name.

- You are not a mistake.

- You were placed here by Me.

- I knew you before you were in your mother's womb.

- I am here.

- Let me fill the vacuum in your heart.

- I see the hidden pain within your heart.

- I will heal your broken heart and bind up your wounds.

- Talk to me and I will listen to you.

Healing is a process. Take what you have learned and experienced in this chapter and allow God to continue His process within you. As you continue to do your part God will do His part! He will accomplish what you cannot. God will take the normal everyday experiences and cause them to be abnormal when you least expect it!

Nonresistant

This chapter introduces the intense training that I had to go through in the midst of the wilderness and the lowest valley of my life. I have identified this segment of my life with an Arabian horse's training of obedience since it parallels with the obedience to God that I had to learn in order to be in the presence of my King!

As I began to see God as my Father who loved me and was with me in all facets of my life I began to acquire a greater understanding of who I was in Him!

Read page 105 in the book *"Touch Me"*.

There are four things to take notice of in the second paragraph.

- I was seeking the Lord for His wisdom to help other people.

If you seek (Wisdom) as for silver and search for skillful and godly Wisdom as for hidden treasures, then you will understand the reverent and worshipful fear of the Lord and find the knowledge of (our omniscient) God. (Proverbs 2:4-5 AMP)

As I was seeking for God's wisdom my heart was open to hear from the Holy Spirit.

- The Holy Spirit announced a major change that was coming into my life.

But when He, the Spirit of Truth (the Truth-giving Spirit) comes, He will guide you into all the Truth (the whole, full Truth). For He will not speak His own message (on His own authority); but He will tell whatever

He hears (from the Father; He will give the message that has been given to Him), and He will announce and declare to you the things that are to come (that will happen in the future). (John 16:13 AMP)

- God spoke in an audible voice while I was in the wilderness in fear of the unknown.

Read and meditate on Genesis 16:1-13.

Because Hagar's mistress Sarah was treating her so badly she escaped into the desert while pregnant with Abraham's child. The Angel of the Lord met her in the midst of the valley of her emotions.

But the Angel of the Lord found her by a spring of water in the wilderness on the road to Shur. (Genesis 16:7 AMP)

I was in the depths of the fear of the unknown not knowing which road to take. God opened up a path to lead and guide me onto His road.

- God gave me the beginning of His instructions in order to accomplish His plan for my life.

The Angel of the Lord said to her, "Go back to your mistress and (humbly) submit to her control. Also the Angel of the Lord said to her, I will multiply your descendants exceedingly, so that they shall not be numbered for multitude. And the Angel of the Lord continued, See now, you are with child and shall bear a son, and shall call his name Ishmael (God hears), because the Lord has heard and paid attention to your affliction. And he (Ishmael) will be as a wild ass among men; his hand will be against every man and every man's hand against him, and he will live to the east and on the borders of all his kinsmen." (Genesis 16:9-12 AMP)

Up to this time in her pregnancy Hagar had submitted to the control of her mistress. However, when the mental distress became too hard she ran away. The Angel of the Lord came to her and told her to return to her mistress and submit. In hearing her cry and seeing her affliction the Angel of the Lord came to her with His mercy. His word imparted encouragement for her and her son's future.

God's word imparted encouragement in the midst of discouragement for my future. This was the beginning of choosing to learn how to humbly submit to God and His will for my life by allowing God to take the reins of my stubborn, self righteous, prideful will.

Read pages 105-106 in the book *"Touch Me".*

The first step in intensive training involved my concentrated effort of taking the time to sit in God's presence and read His word. It was necessary to hear His voice of instructions and obey them.

When you are in tribulation and all these things come upon you, in the latter days you will turn to the Lord your God and be obedient to His voice. (Deuteronomy 4:30 AMP)

I can hear you saying, "How do I recognize the voice of the Holy Spirit over my flesh and the enemy's voice?

- We need to test the spirits by praying for discernment daily.

Beloved, do not put faith in every spirit, but prove (test) the spirits to discover whether they proceed from God; for many false prophets have gone forth into the world. (I John 4:1 AMP)

When I receive a vision, dream or word in my spirit I always ask the Lord for confirmation. If God doesn't confirm this I write it down and tuck it away until God reveals His message to me. I believe that if a dream is from God He will bring the revelation without me trying to figure it out. (Refer to the Introduction on page xxii in the book "Touch Me.")

- I believe first and foremost the voice of the Holy Spirit will be in *agreement* with God's word.

When therefore He had risen from the dead, His disciples remembered that He said this. And so they believed and trusted and relied on the *Scripture* and the *word* (message) *Jesus had spoken*. (John 2:22 AMP)

- The Holy Spirit will speak words of life that will bring ***comfort*** and ***revive*** your soul.

This is my *comfort* and consolation in my affliction: that Your word has *revived me* and given me life. (Psalm 119:50 AMP)

- The Holy Spirit will bring ***conviction*** not ***condemnation.***

Every Scripture is God-breathed (given by His inspiration) and profitable for instruction, for reproof and *conviction* of sin, for correction of error and discipline in obedience, (and) for training in righteousness (in holy living, in conformity to God's will in thought, purpose, and action), so that the man of God may be complete and proficient, well fitted and thoroughly equipped for every good work. (II Timothy 3:16-17 AMP)

Therefore, (there is) now no *condemnation* (no adjudging guilty of wrong) for those who are in Christ Jesus, who live (and) walk not after the dictates of the flesh, but after the dictates of the Spirit. (Romans 8:1 AMP)

Condemnation commands our minds to be tormented. The Holy Spirit's conviction imparts life in our spirit and gives us the desire to follow His command!

I began to draw near to God with an honest and sincere heart placing my confidence and trust in His love and power. **He drew near to me** with His wisdom, goodness and faithfulness in beginning to cleanse and purify my heart and mind.

Let us all come forward and draw near with true (honest and sincere) hearts in unqualified assurance and absolute conviction engendered by faith (by that leaning of the entire human personality on God in absolute trust and confidence in His power, wisdom, and goodness), having our hearts sprinkled and purified from a guilty (evil) conscience and our bodies cleansed with pure water. (Hebrews 10:22 AMP)

In the midst of this very difficult trial I began to learn these lessons:

- Even though satan showed up with a truck load of promises I still had the **choice** to say yes or no! When I said no to satan's promises and yes to God's promises, **He kept my feet from slipping**.

For the Lord shall be your confidence, firm and strong, and shall keep your foot from being caught (in a trap or some hidden danger). (Proverbs 3:26 AMP)

- I knew that God was my Creator and Savior but now He was becoming my **Lord** and **Master** in the midst of the pain and suffering.

Ye call me Master and Lord: and ye say well; for so I am. (John 13:13 KJV)

God was no longer a Bible God that I read about and heard of for so many years while attending church. He became my personal God who I could have an intimate one on one conversation with daily!

- God was calling me to confront an issue however; I was in fear of the confrontation. **God showed me that He was not my task master** and didn't give me this assignment to burden or oppress me. As His love surrounded me I no longer felt intimidated by other people through the fearful thoughts from the enemy. I realized that **satan was the real taskmaster who had convinced me for over thirty years that it was God!** (Refer to image on page 106 in the book *"Touch Me".)*

So they set over the (Israelites) taskmasters to afflict and oppress them with (increased) burdens. And (the Israelites) built Pithom and Rameses as store cities for Pharaoh. (Exodus 1:11 AMP)

I am reminded of a program on television many years ago called, "I've got a secret!" Each person portrayed the real character and other people had to decide who was telling the truth! When God showed me His love this was a pivotal moment for me. I saw the real taskmaster stand up! Satan's secret lie was no longer hidden!

Read pages 107-111 in the book *"Touch Me".*

- I began to trust that my God knew what was best for me even though I couldn't understand why I had to endure this trial.

Commit your way to the Lord (roll and repose each care of your load on Him); trust (lean on, rely on, and be confident) also in Him and He will bring it to pass. (Psalm 37:5 AMP)

As I spent time with God daily my prayers began to change. I was no longer committed to doing it my way but became committed to obeying His way.

- I could no longer fill the void in my heart with material things since they were being stripped away. God showed me that He wanted to be **everything** that I needed.

And set your minds and keep them set on what is above (the higher things), not on the things that are on the earth. (Colossians 3:2 AMP)

When I set my mind on God He became larger and my problems became smaller.

- God became my **husband** and filled the emptiness and loneliness in my heart.

For your Maker is your Husband the Lord of hosts is His name and the Holy One of Israel is your Redeemer; the God of the whole earth He is called. (Isaiah 54:5)

- Until I found myself standing in a welfare line for food stamps I hadn't realized what other people experience. Even though we were not wealthy I had never experienced lack of food, clothing and the necessities of life. I was turned down for food stamps since we had a house and a business. God showed me that He was my **provider** in ways that I couldn't think or imagine!

Read Philippians 4:19 on page 107 in the book *"Touch Me"*.

I had been a Home Interiors displayer before the marriage separation. I was waiting to receive a recruiting check from the company. One day I was with a couple that had been asking God to provide a certain amount for an appliance. I was not aware of their prayer or need when the Holy Spirit spoke a certain amount that He wanted me to give them. It was the same amount I would receive for recruiting other displayers. When the check came I was amazed at the peace I had in giving it to them when I so desperately needed it.

Now to Him who, by (in consequence of) the (action of His) power that is at work within us, is able to (carry out His purpose and) do superabundantly, far over and above all that we (dare) ask or think (infinitely beyond our highest prayers, desires, thoughts, hopes, or dreams). (Ephesians 3:20 AMP)

God met their need through me and then met my needs through others! As I handed all that God had instructed me to give He met my needs in ways that I could never think or imagine. You can never out give the Lord!

- I learned to trust Him for my physical and spiritual nourishment in my desert experience.

In the evening quails came up and covered the camp; and in the morning the dew lay round about the camp. And when the dew had gone, behold, upon the face of the wilderness there lay a fine, round and flake like thing, as fine as hoarfrost on the ground. When the Israelites saw it, they said one to another, "Manna, (What is it)?" For they did not know what it was. And Moses said to them, "This is the bread which the Lord has given you to eat." (Exodus 16:13-15 AMP)

Jesus replied, "I am the Bread of Life. He who comes to Me will never be hungry, and he who believes in and cleaves to and trusts in and relies on Me will never thirst any more (at any time)." (John 6:35 AMP)

As I prayed for fresh manna daily one day I heard the Holy Spirit say, "My children are begging for a piece of bread when I have already given them the loaf!" Jesus is the loaf!

- I began to learn that God was my burden bearer. As I gave these burdens to Him the weight was lifted off my shoulders. (Read Psalm 68:19 on page 108 in the book *"Touch Me".)*

Come to Me, all you who labor and are heavy-laden and overburdened, and I will cause you to rest. (I will ease and relieve and refresh your souls. Take My yoke upon you and learn of Me, for I am gentle (meek) and humble (lowly) in heart, and you will find rest (ʰrelief and ease and refreshment and recreation and blessed quiet) for your souls.

For My yoke is wholesome (useful, good—not harsh, hard, sharp, or pressing, but comfortable, gracious, and pleasant), and My burden is light and easy to be borne. (Matthew 11:28-30 AMP)

- God delivered me from the shame of divorce when I gave Him the burden of guilt and repented of my sins of self righteousness and spiritual pride.

And that I may (actually) be found and known as in Him, not having any (self-achieved) righteousness that can be called my own, based on my obedience to the Law's demands (ritualistic uprightness and supposed right standing with God thus acquired), but possessing that (genuine righteousness) which comes through faith in Christ (the Anointed One), the (truly) right standing with God, which comes from God by (saving) faith. (Philippians 3:9 AMP)

- One day I was walking the streets of Lancaster city. A young man looking very unkempt with long hair crossed the walk ahead of me. In those days they were called hippies and many people looked down upon them. I am sorry to say I was one of those people! Suddenly I felt God's overwhelming love for him. When I experienced this agape love for him I felt and realized the agape (unconditional) love God has for me. I felt joy in my spirit as this became a major turning point in my life from being self righteous to seeking God's righteousness!

He refreshes and restores my life (myself); He leads me in the paths of righteousness (uprightness and right standing with Him—not for my earning it, but) for His name's sake. (Psalm 23:3 AMP)

I experienced the power of the Holy Spirit that brought hope in the midst of the sadness in my soul. (Refer to image on page 108 in the book *"Touch Me".)*

May the God of your hope so fill you with all joy and peace in believing (through the experience of your faith) that by the power of the Holy Spirit you may abound and be overflowing (bubbling over) with hope. (Romans 15:13 AMP)

When the Holy Spirit gave me a song my soul began to flourish in the midst of the grief in my life.

- I learned what delight yourself in the Lord really means. (Refer to Psalm 37:4 and Greek meaning of delight on page 109 in the book *"Touch Me".)*

I always thought that as long as I was enjoying God by praising and worshipping Him all the desires of my heart would be fulfilled. When I didn't receive those desires that I thought I should have, I became frustrated with this scripture. However, when I went through this trial He showed me the only way we can truly enjoy God is to be soft and pliable before HIM!

As I allowed my heart to be soft and pliable for God's use, I began to experience the true joy in making my life about HIM and not me! My desires were no longer about my selfishness but were about His selflessness.

- I learned to trust the Lord with my children and know that He had the best for them even if I didn't understand HIS BEST!

As long as I held onto what I thought was best I couldn't see GOD'S BEST for my son. When I told God how much I loved my son, His reply was "I love my son too!" At that moment our hearts connected and I gave Him my son. This word from the Lord has made a major impact in praying for my children and grandchildren.

- As I began to obey God even when I didn't understand or revel in His plan I experienced more of His presence in ways that I couldn't think or imagine. As He began to reveal more of Himself to me I began to want more of Him and less of me.

When you are in tribulation and all these things come upon you, in the latter days you will turn to the Lord your God and be obedient to His voice. For the Lord your God is a merciful God; He will not fail you or destroy you or forget the covenant of your fathers, which He swore to them. (Deuteronomy 4:30-31 AMP)

Obedience is the key that unlocks the door to the Holy Spirit's presence.

- As I began to learn that He truly was my Abba Father I learned to crawl up on my Daddy's lap as His little girl and tell Him where I was hurting.

Some of you may have a problem with seeing God as your Father or Daddy. I have heard arguments against this since some Christians feel that it's not giving respect to a Holy God. Still others of you may have been so wounded by your earthly father that it's hard to envision your Heavenly Father as loving and gentle. I am reminded of a television show years ago called, "Father Knows Best!" In this show the father was greatly respected even when the children didn't always agree. Yet, they knew he always knew best for them even better than they knew for themselves. He didn't abuse them with his authority but treated them with dignity, respect and love. When he didn't agree with them he didn't berate them or make them feel insecure. He encouraged them to mature by allowing them to make their own choices. When they made the wrong choices he felt badly for them knowing that consequences would have to follow. The children knew they could come to their father without being judged or criticized for their emotions. He always took time out of his busy schedule to listen intently. He had a great sense of humor and laughed with his children. When his children admitted their sins with broken hearts he forgave them and never brought up these sins again. When they broke something they brought it to their daddy to fix it. They played games together as a family and enjoyed each other's company. Their father saw in them what they couldn't see because they weren't mature enough.

Maybe some of you have or had an earthly father like this one. I believe that it's a lot easier for you to relate to God as your Father. How much greater is your Heavenly Father than your earthly father?

If you then, evil as you are, know how to give good and advantageous gifts to your children, how much more will your Father Who is in heaven (perfect as He is) give good and advantageous things to those who keep on asking Him! (Matthew 7:11 AMP)

There is no gift on this earth that compares to the gift our Father has given us in Himself!

At that time the disciples came up and asked Jesus, "Who then is (really) the greatest in the kingdom of heaven?" And He called a little child to Himself and put him in the midst of them. (Matthew 18:1-2 AMP)

Read Matthew 18:3-4 on page 111 in the book *"Touch Me"*.

A little child comes willingly to a loving daddy with open arms expecting him to pick her/him up and place her/him on his lap and hold her/him. They are not self sufficient but trust, rely and cling to their father's sufficiency.

- I had not only read about the mercies of the Lord in His word but now I truly experienced His mercy in the midst of the mercilessness from the enemy. (Refer to Lamentations 3:21-23 on page 111 in the book *"Touch Me".)*

- One night in our prayer meeting with the Promise Land Ministries team we observed a huge circle around the moon above our home as everyone was leaving. My first thought was this is God's circle of love. I had never seen this before and didn't realize that it was called a halo. I dismissed my first thought until God brought this scripture to my attention as I was writing this guide.

I hate all this silly religion, but you, God, I trust. I'm leaping and singing in the circle of your love; you saw my pain, you disarmed my tormentors, You didn't leave me in their clutches but gave me room to breathe. (Psalm 31:7-10 Message)

This scripture says it all in this segment of the guide as I learned God's lessons of love.

In reviewing these seventeen lessons what lesson impacted you the most? Share them with each other.

What lessons have you learned in the midst of a trial?

Read page 112 in the book **"Touch Me"**.

In this next season it was time for God to turn up the heat to rid my soul of more impurities. There were days the fire got so hot that I thought I couldn't stand it any longer. One particular day I was crying out to the Lord and received this vision. I saw Jesus holding a jewel in His hand. He breathed on it and took a cloth and began polishing it.

Then He looked into it as though it were a mirror. He couldn't quite see His reflection so He said it needed more time.

Read the scripture in Isaiah 64:8 on page 113 in the book **"Touch Me"**.

Let's linger here for a moment and let's be honest with ourselves and God.

Do you see yourself as the clay and God your Potter or God as the clay that has to fit into your plan?

Notice the pain in my past would be the catalyst that would propel me into God's plan for my future. Therefore like clay, I had to go through this process of being hammered, rolled out, straightened and placed into a hot burning furnace in order to be a reflection of God's love.

Read the scripture in Zechariah 9:16 on page 113 in the book **"Touch Me"**.

Just as an artist pictures a masterpiece in his mind, I believe our God has a picture of us in His mind and knows what we need to go through in order to become His precious masterpiece shining with His crown of love.

Refer to the image on page 113 in the book **"Touch Me"**.

I am reminded of the story of Adam and Eve. Imagine walking every day holding hands with God and not having any cares of this world. God owns the cattle on a thousand hills and gave it all to them with the exception of one tree. I believe all of their needs and wants were fulfilled by God. But most of all they had His presence of love daily. We don't know what God spoke to them daily but I believe that He told them how much He loved them. God is not just a God of love. He is love! I remember when I was going through one of these rough times in my life and was talking with God about it. He spoke this into my spirit, "You could have it worse. You could be without me."

Eve was tempted by the serpent and ate the fruit of the forbidden tree of the knowledge of good and evil. Then she offered it to Adam. One day I was thinking about what this world would be like if Eve hadn't listened to the serpent and fallen into satan's web of seduction. What difference would it have made for us? What could she have done to prevent this?

Why didn't God's love for her over power the temptation? Why didn't she run away from the tempter and run into God's arms of love? Was she afraid to tell God of this temptation? Did she think that He would be disappointed in her? Up until this time she had not seen evil since she only knew the goodness of God. So . . . in all God's goodness why didn't she recognize the evil? I believe it began when the serpent placed **doubt** in her mind that caused her to dismiss God's word.

Now the serpent was more crafty than any of the wild animals the LORD God had made. He said to the woman, "Did God really say, 'You must not eat from any tree in the garden'?" The woman said to the serpent, "We may eat fruit from the trees in the garden, but God did say, 'You must not eat fruit from the tree that is in the middle of the garden, and you must not touch it, or you will die.'" (Genesis 3:1-3 NIV)

Satan masquerades as an angel of light.

And it is no wonder, for satan himself masquerades as an angel of light. (II Corinthians 11:14 AMP)

"You will not certainly die," the serpent said to the woman. "For God knows that when you eat from it your eyes will be opened, and you will be like God, knowing good and evil." (Genesis 3:4-5 NIV)

God says His word is eternal!

Your word O Lord is eternal. It stands firm in the heavens. (Psalm 119:89 NIV)

I will not violate my covenant or alter what my lips have uttered. (Psalm 89:34 NIV)

When Eve looked at the tree she could only see how good and pleasant it was for food. It was delightful to look at and a tree to be desired to make her wise.

And when the woman saw that the tree was good (suitable, pleasant) for food and that it was delightful to look at, and a tree to be desired in order to make one wise, she took of its fruit and ate; and she gave some also to her husband, and he ate. (Genesis 3:6 AMP)

God did not create Eve to be an angel. He made her a human being with weaknesses to give to Him so He could perfect them. As I read this scripture I felt that because the doubt was planted in her heart by the serpent she believed satan's word over God's. I really like homemade chocolate chip cookies and love to smell that wonderful aroma. Especially when they are fresh out of the oven I hear them calling my name. I hear, "Oh! Just eat one . . . and then . . . two won't hurt. Three is a bit much but tomorrow you won't eat them or January is coming up . . . then I'll diet!" Afterwards, I find myself being upset that I ate too many. Satan sits on my shoulder and entices me. After I yield to the temptation he sits on the other shoulder and condemns me. Eve yielded to the temptation and was enticed by the enemy of curiosity and pride.

So . . . how do we stay free from satan's web of seduction?

Fred and I went to the shore for a couple of days to celebrate our twenty-third anniversary. While we were down at Ocean City, Maryland there was a hurricane watch and a tropical storm warning. The waves were bigger than we had ever seen them in the twenty-three years of traveling to the shore. As I sat on the beach I heard the words **"*Catch the wave*"** in my spirit. God began to show me to observe the people on the beach. As I watched I realized that He was showing me why many of His children do not and will not jump into His wave of love!

As I observed all of the people in the water and on the beach this is what I saw:

- Some were staying away from not only the waves but from the water itself. They were sitting in their chairs under umbrellas. They were totally comfortable to sit out on the beach and not venture into the water which would place them out of their comfort zones.

Most of us do not like coming out of our comfort zones. Depending upon how we have grown up or been taught we like life to be the same. I think about the differences in traditional and contemporary worship services. If you are used to one of them you don't like change and it's very hard to accept it. Many people are sitting on the **seat of complacency** feeling satisfied with themselves thinking they are fine. They have taken the first step in asking Jesus into their heart but have not taken the next step to have a relationship with Him.

For the backsliding of the simple shall slay them, and the careless ease of (*self-confident*) fools shall destroy them. (Proverbs 1:32 AMP)

- Some would just get in and get their feet wet . . . . some would go in up to their waist and some to their shoulders. They would only venture so far but not go any further.

I remember when the Jesus Movement swept through our area with many fresh encounters with the Lord that included receiving the Baptism of the Holy Spirit. Some people were **afraid** that it might be from the devil. Actually that is what I was told from a minister who really believed that. I remember when I went to my first meeting and saw women raising their hands. It felt so strange yet a part of me wanted to get my feet wet . . . just a little but not too much!

There is no fear in love (dread does not exist), but full-grown (complete, perfect) love turns *fear* out of doors and expels every trace of terror! For fear brings with it the thought of punishment, and (so) he who is afraid has not reached the full maturity of love (is not yet grown into love's complete perfection). (I John 4:18 AMP)

- Because the waves became high enough we saw some surfers riding the waves. They received the **thrill** of it but not the full impact!

As time went on I received the Baptism of the Holy Spirit and began watching some people who were caught up in the emotion and the **thrill of the gifts** of the Holy Spirit but not knowing the Lord who is the **Giver** of the gifts!

Without having seen Him, you love Him; though you do not (even) now see Him, you believe in Him and exult and *thrill* with inexpressible and glorious (triumphant, heavenly) joy. (I Peter 1:8 AMP)

The Holy Spirit spoke this to me when I was going through this particular trial while learning His lessons of love. He said, "My people would love me if they knew me."

- I noticed that some people weren't interested in the waves. They just continued to do their own thing.

There are people that have no interest in the plan God has for them and do not want God messing up their plans. So they continue to feed their flesh and not their spirit.

For those who are according to the flesh and are *controlled* by its unholy desires set their minds on and pursue those things which gratify the flesh, but those who are according to the Spirit and are controlled by the desires of the Spirit set their minds on and seek those things which gratify the (Holy)Spirit. (Romans 8:5 AMP)

But you are not living the life of the flesh, you are living the life of the Spirit, if the (Holy) Spirit of God (really) dwells within you (directs and *controls* you). But if anyone does not possess the (Holy) Spirit of Christ,

he is none of His (he does not belong to Christ, is not truly a child of God). (Romans 8:9 AMP)

One night in a dream I saw two silhouettes that looked entirely different. The first one was so skinny that it resembled a skeleton. The other one was filled out and had a light of radiance around it. As I prayed about it the Holy Spirit revealed the meaning to me. The skeleton represented my flesh. The filled out radiant one represented my spirit.

When you feed your spirit with God's word you starve your flesh! However, when you ignore God's word you starve your spirit and feed your flesh!

- Some people stood back too far missing the waves while others jumped in.

When my girlfriend told me about the Baptism of the Holy Spirit and shared her experience with me about the Lord, I stood back and just **observed** her life. Eventually the Lord placed a mirror in front of me and showed me that I was self righteous. Observing the love of Jesus in her is what drew me to want what she had.

If anyone thinks himself to be religious (piously *observant* of the external duties of his faith) and does not bridle his tongue but deludes his own heart, this person's religious service is worthless (futile, barren) (James 1:26 AMP)

- Still others were more interested in **pleasures** and were not looking at the waves before them.

Some people are into their **pleasures** and accumulating stuff in this world that they haven't considered their life here on earth let alone their life eternally.

(Here) on earth you have abandoned yourselves to soft (prodigal) living and to (the *pleasures* of) self-indulgence and self-gratification. You have fattened your hearts in a day of slaughter. (James 5:5 AMP)

- Others got **tired** fighting the waves and gave up.

Sometimes the battle seems so tough. The flesh wants to give up fighting the enemy and the web of discouragement comes in. The spirit is willing but the **flesh is weak**. When you jump into God's wave you become immersed in His love that keeps your focus on Him and not the enemy of your soul.

All of you must keep awake (give strict attention, be cautious and active) and watch and pray, that you may not come into temptation. The spirit indeed is willing, but the *flesh is weak*. (Matthew 26:41 AMP)

- Some people were standing back taking pictures of other people in the water.

There are people that think it is okay for you but leave me out of the picture. They simply are **not interested** in knowing God and are completely satisfied with their life.

For the others all seek (to advance) their own interests, not those of Jesus Christ (the Messiah). (Philippians 2:21 AMP)

Their moral understanding is darkened and their reasoning is beclouded. (They are) alienated (estranged, self-banished) from the life of God (with no share in it; this is) because of the ignorance (the want of knowledge and perception, the willful blindness) that is deep-seated in them, due to their *hardness of heart* (to the insensitiveness of their moral nature). (Ephesians 4:18 AMP)

- Some people simply stood back and thought the others were crazy for being in the water.

When the Baptism of the Holy Spirit was introduced to our area in the 70's some thought those people were Jesus freaks and stood back and **judged** and **criticized** them. Many people did not understand God's love because they had grown up hearing all about His judgment.

But since it is merely a question (of doctrine) about words and names and your own law, see to it yourselves; I decline to be a *judge* of such matters and I have no intention of trying such cases. (Acts 18:15 AMP)

Are you not discriminating among your own and becoming *critics* and *judges* with wrong motives? (James 2:4 AMP)

***Judge* not (neither pronouncing judgment nor subjecting to censure), and you will not be *judged*; do not condemn and pronounce guilty, and you will not be condemned and pronounced guilty; acquit and forgive and release (give up resentment, let it drop), and you will be acquitted and forgiven and released. (Luke 6:37 AMP)**

- Some would receive the full impact of the wave but when the waves broke others only received a ripple.

Even though there were people who wanted to experience God's love they settled for a ripple since they didn't want to be looked upon as a Jesus freak!

Elijah came near to all the people and said, "How long will you halt and limp between *two opinions*? If the Lord is God, follow Him! But if Baal, then follow him." And the people did not answer him a word. (I Kings 18:21 AMP)

- Some walked near the waves but fear held them back from jumping in.

Fear plays a major part of not being able to come close to God. Actually why is that? I believe the ***darkness in our heart*** wants to hide but God knows what is in our heart. The closer we walk with the Lord the more He uncovers or reveals the darkness in our heart and mind which brings about conviction of the Holy Spirit which leads to repentance and frees us.

When His disciples heard this, many of them said, "This is a hard and difficult and strange saying (an offensive and unbearable message). Who can stand to hear it?" (Who can be expected to listen to such teaching?) (John 6:60 AMP)

The heart is deceitful above all things, and it is exceedingly perverse and corrupt and severely, mortally sick! Who can know it (perceive, understand, be acquainted with his own heart and mind)? (Jeremiah 17:9 AMP)

- Sometimes I noticed people all by themselves.

People choose to be loners for different reasons. Some have been wounded by others and find themselves not being able to trust again. Still others have carried bitterness, resentment and unforgiveness for so long that they have allowed their hearts to harden towards other people. Some people feel they don't need anyone in their lives.

For I see that you are in the gall of bitterness and in a bond forged by iniquity (to fetter souls). (Acts 8:23 AMP)

Let all bitterness and indignation and wrath (passion, rage, bad temper) and resentment (anger, animosity) and quarreling (brawling, clamor, contention) and slander (evil-speaking, abusive or blasphemous language) be banished from you, with all malice (spite, ill will, or baseness of any kind). (Ephesians 4:31 AMP)

Still others have unanswered prayers that have caused them to shun God instead of the evil in their life.

- I noticed some people carrying towels on their shoulders while walking on the beach.

The towels represented burdens that people carry. When we carry the weight of the world upon our shoulders it causes us to be stoop shouldered and unable to fight the enemy of our soul. God did not create us to carry burdens but to give the burdens to Him!

Blessed be the Lord, Who bears our burdens and carries us day by day, even the God Who is our salvation! (Psalm 68:19 AMP)

Casting the whole of your care (all your anxieties, all your worries, all your concerns, once and for all) on Him, for He cares for you affectionately and cares about you watchfully. (I Peter 5:7 AMP)

- Others deliberately walked away from other people so they wouldn't get wet.

Some people do not want any part of the love message since they see God's judgment and not His love! They have not gotten the message in their heart of the grace that God has given us through Jesus dying on the cross to bring us abundant life with Him here on earth and in heaven.

For the Lord God is a Sun and Shield; the Lord bestows (present) grace and favor and (future) glory (honor, splendor, and heavenly bliss)! No good thing will He withhold from those who walk uprightly. (Psalm 84:11 AMP)

All are justified and made upright and in right standing with God, freely and gratuitously by His grace (His unmerited favor and mercy), through the redemption which is (provided) in Christ Jesus. (Romans 3:24 AMP)

But then Law came in, (only) to expand and increase the trespass (making it more apparent and exciting opposition). But where sin increased and abounded, grace (God's unmerited favor) has surpassed it and increased the more and superabounded, so that, (just) as sin has reigned in death, (so) grace (His unearned and undeserved favor) might reign also through righteousness (right standing with God) which issues in eternal life through Jesus Christ (the Messiah, the Anointed One) our Lord. (Romans 5:20-21 AMP)

The day before the rip tides became too dangerous many children were playing and jumping in the water. I watched as some children reached out their hand for their parent and giggled as their Mom or Dad's strong hand held them up with the continuing waves. Afterwards, some children took hold of each other's hands with their heads held high while playing in the water with great excitement. I was delighted as I watched the children laughing and having a great time. I realized this is how God sees us. We are His children. When He sees us reach out for His hand He gladly holds us up with the strength of His hand. When we experience an intimate personal relationship with God we are able to take each other's hands in love and acceptance of the differences in our Christian doctrine and beliefs. We can hold our heads high since we are the princes and princesses of our Almighty King!

God is calling us all to come to Him like a little child and to jump into His arms of LOVE!

Whoever will humble himself therefore and become like this little child (trusting, lowly, loving, forgiving) is greatest in the kingdom of heaven. (Matthew 18:4 AMP)

Some of you may feel that it's too late and you have gone too far. Review and discuss these webs. Some of you may know what web you have been in and others may not have that revelation. After you review these webs I would like to encourage you to ask the Lord what has been holding you back from experiencing His love. Will you choose satan's web or God's love?

- Web of doubting God's word.

- Web of complacency (Sitting on the seat of complacency.)

- Web of fear of an encounter with God.

- Web of the thrill of the gifts of the Spirit vs. knowing God who is the Giver.

- Web of flesh/spirit controlled.

- Web of self righteousness.

- Web of pleasures (Seeking own pleasures.)

- Web of discouragement (Tired of fighting the enemy.)

- Web of disinterest in God.

- Web of criticism and judgment.

- Web of confusion (Tossed between two opinions.)

- Web of darkness in the heart.

- Web of bitterness, resentment and unforgiveness. (Unanswered prayers.)

- Web of Burdens.

- Web of the denial of God's grace.

So I'm going to ask you to pray this with me. God is here right now to touch your heart and set you free from satan's web of deception.

Father, as I have studied this lesson on satan's webs I realize that I have been in a web of (name the web). Forgive me for doubting your word that has caused me to get into these webs. I give you the unbelief that is within my heart and mind that has caused me to remain in satan's web of deception. I ask that you reveal any other webs that I have not been aware of. Help me to have the desire to walk in your waves of love and be immersed in you every day. In Jesus' Name. Amen.

Are you ready to be a part of a sudden, rapid, widespread explosion of God's love?

The Breaker (the Messiah) will go up before them. They will break through, pass in through the gate and go out through it, and their King will pass on before them, the Lord at their head. (Micah 2:13 AMP)

So . . . what happens when you jump into His waves of love?

The Holy Spirit spoke this during one of my quiet times with Him.

"Let me steep you in my love. I have so much for you. My love is wider than the greatest width, deeper than the deepest depth and higher than the highest high on this earth. Let me soak you in my love. As you soak in my love you will teach others how to soak. As you soak in my love I remove all the impurities. I change what you cannot change. I heal those deep embedded wounds. My child I want to show you the importance of soaking in my presence. All fears dissipate in my presence. Calloused hearts become softened."

Afterwards, I received this vision. He showed me a hand that looked dirty, grimy and covered with grease. I saw the hand soaking in a solution in order to remove the grease and then God began to speak to me on what His love does.

So I'm going to ask you to place instrumental music on and listen to God's heart while the group leader says the following. If you are not in a group setting, place the music on and say this out loud to yourself. Allow God to steep you in His love letter!

"My Love"

My love *chips* away at the hate of this world. My love *covers* the wrongs done to you. My love *quenches* your thirst. My love *fills* the void in your heart. My love *rekindles* the fire in your spirit. My love *removes* the pain and sorrow in your life. My love *wraps* around you like a cloak. My love *brings* forgiveness where you have unforgiveness. My love *takes* the importance off of you and places it onto others. My love *generates* more love to others. My love *satisfies* the hunger in your soul. My love *sees* the imperfections and perfects the weaknesses. My love *dissipates* the fear and brings peace. My love *shelters* you in the storms of life. My love *speaks* to others without judgment or criticism. My love *gives* up the right to hurt the other person back. My love *overlooks* the insults and seeks reconciliation. My love *abounds* where strife and conflict had control. My love *paralyzes* greed and brings generosity. My love *prevails* over injustice. My love *seizes* the violence and destruction. My love *carries* joy to a tormented mind. My love *brings* healing to a self inflicted injury. My love *captivates* the beauty in others. My love *comforts* in your time of need. My love *flashes* destruction on the enemy's plot.

My love *removes* the shackles and *restores* the years eaten by pain and suffering. My love *untangles* the web of deceit. My love *rebuilds* what the web of destruction destroyed. My love *seeks* peace where there is conflict. My love *hurls* the iniquities into the depths of the sea. My love *revives* the heart and *heals* the embittered soul. My love *dries* up the tears of pain and anguish. My love *pursues* the enemy into darkness and shines the light of my goodness. My love *pardons* sin and forgives the transgression. My love *delights* to show mercy and compassion.

My love *guides* you onto my path. My love *teaches* you in the valleys. My love *guards* your mouth and tongue from calamity. My love *transforms* the human heart and mind. My love *conveys* the message of acceptance in the midst of man's rejection.

My love *overcomes* the hurdles. My love *delights* to show mercy and compassion. My love *sings and rejoices* over you.

One morning I was sitting outside in our backyard listening to many different kinds of birds singing beautiful melodies in unison. At that moment the Holy Spirit asked me this question. He said, "My child, do you hear the birds singing? They wake up every morning rejoicing and praising me. That is how I want my children to wake up!"

The following morning I went back to the same area in our back yard and sat in silence waiting for God to speak to me. As I sat there I could only hear the dead silence. Not a bird was singing and my mind was replaying some painful incidents in my past. I began to tell God that sometimes I wish that He would just take me to heaven. I told Him that I get tired of dealing with the same old same olds in my life. Suddenly I found myself praying this simple prayer.

Lord, change me. Let me not look at how much love I receive from others but how much love I give to others.

I opened my Bible to Zephaniah 3:17 that says, "The Lord your God is in the midst of you; a Mighty One, a Savior who saves. He will rest in silent satisfaction and in His love He will be silent and make no mention (of past sins or even recall them). He will exalt over you with singing."

I asked the Lord this question. "Do you really sing over me?"

The Holy Spirit spoke this to me. "I am taking you on a quest to experience more of my love. Your love for me has been tested many years. Now it's time for you to experience my love greater than you could imagine. My love will begin to pour upon you in places you least expect. Yesterday I showed you my love in the birds singing. Today I show you my love in silence as I give my song to you."

Suddenly this song rose up in my spirit as He sang this to me. I could hardly write it down as the tears were falling down my cheeks and His love was surrounding me. God gave this to me to share with you.

This is what your Father sings over you. (Sing this to the music of "You are my sunshine").

"You are my sunshine, my lovely sunshine. When your skies are cloudy or when they're blue. I want you to know my child how much I love you. I will always be here for you."

"You are my sunshine, my precious sunshine. No matter what you've done or didn't do. But I know my child that I'll always love you and rejoice and sing over you."

"You are my sunshine, my beautiful sunshine. I didn't create you to be blue. So please remember I'm right here waiting. Everyday I'm watching over you."

I had the excitement of a little child that had been given a very special gift.

What will you choose today? Are you lost and feeling alone? God is here to show you the way out.

We receive gifts from our friends and family for Christmas, birthdays and so forth. As you unwrap the gifts from others remember that God has placed His gifts within you. However, until you jump into His love and receive His healing many of those gifts will stay dormant.

Ask and it will be given to you; seek and you will find; knock and the door will be opened to you. For everyone who asks receives; the one who seeks finds; and to the one who knocks, the door will be opened. (Matthew 7:7-8 NIV)

Are you asking, seeking and knocking?

Read pages 114-115 in the book *"Touch Me"*.

Some days our faith is at an all time high and other days it is so low that we wonder what happened. When our faith is high we are saying, "Okay God bring on the challenges!" When our faith is lower we say, "Not today Lord. I don't want any more pain."

We don't like challenges that are painful. We can't see the end of our life but we can know that God has good plans for us and promises to walk with us through the journey.

What challenges are you facing?

When God spoke through a lady to tell me that I was called here I asked God to change my heart since I didn't have any desire to stay. Maybe you have moved to another area that you haven't been able to call your home for many years. Perhaps you are in a situation like I was and have been crying out for many years for God to take you back home. Ask God to change your heart and bring contentment wherever He takes you.

But godliness with contentment is great gain. (I Timothy 6:6 NIV)

When we are secure in God's love for us we will experience our journey with contentment in Him no matter where He places us.

Refer to the image on page 116 in the book *"Touch Me"*.

It's so easy to see the sin in other people but it's much harder to see it in ourselves. When I began to make my life about God and not about myself, He began to free me in areas of my heart that I wasn't aware of. As the Holy Spirit revealed the darkness in my heart I ***admitted*** it, ***repented*** and ***asked God to change my heart.***

Read pages 116-117 in the book *"Touch Me"*.

Refer to the image on page 117 in the book *"Touch Me"*.

Inclination brings ***declaration*** which leads to God's ***revelations*** that cause His ***manifestations***.

Whoa! That's a mouth full . . . but what does it mean? Let's linger on this statement for a little while.

First of all, let's look at the definition of *inclination* along with Psalm 78:1 and Isaiah 26:3.

The Hebrew word for **incline** is *natah* (naw-taw) which means to stretch forth or bend away. (Strong's)

When I was attending some ministry classes I wanted to hear every word the teacher was saying. Sometimes I had to make the effort to stretch my body by leaning forward in my chair to draw closer so I could hear more clearly. I had to deliberately make the effort to close my mind off to other thoughts and distractions around me so I could concentrate on the lesson from the teacher. As I listened intently to the teacher I would gain more knowledge and understanding of the teacher's heart. At the end of the class the teacher would give us homework to review from the lesson we studied.

When we attend God's classes making the effort to stretch with our whole heart, soul and mind to hear God's heart we will begin to hear with our spiritual ears and gain His wisdom and understanding of His word.

Refer to page 118 in the book *"Touch Me"*.

As I began to bind each one in Jesus' Name I thanked God they were no longer there since whatever I bind on earth is bound in heaven and whatever I loose on earth is loosed in heaven.

I will give you the keys of the kingdom of heaven; and whatever you bind (*declare* to be improper and unlawful) on earth must be what is already bound in heaven; and whatever you loose (*declare* lawful) on earth must be what is already loosed in heaven. (Matthew 16:19 AMP)

One of the synonyms for lawful is endorse. Therefore, when we bind the spirit of fear and loose the spirit of faith in Jesus' Name Jesus' official stamp of approval is on it!

In my first marriage we had a used car dealership. One of my tasks in the office was notary work. When someone purchased a vehicle from us it was no longer ours but now was transferred in their name. It was unlawful for us to hold onto the vehicle since they paid for it. However, it was not official until I placed my notary stamp and endorsed it with my signature on the motor vehicle form.

When we pray in Jesus' Name we transfer those burdens to Him. He then endorses His official signature and stamps His approval on our prayers in heaven.

One of the Hebrew words for **declare** is **nagad** *(naw-gad)* which means to announce (always by word of mouth to one present), profess, speak, stand boldly out opposite. (Strong's)

Read Numbers 14:6-30 AMP

Joshua and Caleb looked at the Promised Land filled with God's goodness. They saw the giants but believed God would help them fight the giants. However, the other Israelites listened to satan's words of fear instead of taking God at His word and were ready to stone Joshua and Caleb. At that moment God appeared at the meeting with all of the Israelites. God spoke to Moses about the contempt and unbelief of the Israelites. God was tired of their disrespectful and arrogant attitudes towards Him and His people and was ready to destroy them with a plague. However, Moses declared to the Lord what God had declared about Himself!

And now, I pray You, let the power of my Lord be great, as You have promised, saying, "The Lord is long-suffering and slow to anger, and abundant in mercy and loving-kindness, forgiving iniquity and transgression; but He will by no means clear the guilty, visiting the iniquity of the fathers upon the children, upon the third and fourth generation. Pardon, I pray You, the iniquity of this people according to the greatness of Your mercy and loving-kindness, just as You have forgiven (them) from Egypt until now. (verses 17-19)

And the Lord said, "I have pardoned according to your word." (verse 20)

Moses declared God's word that united with God's heart! God listened to Moses' heart when He spoke God's word and declared release from the punishment of a plague for the Israelites.

Refer to image on page 118 in the book ***"Touch Me"***.

Let's take a look at the difference between our selfish human love v/s God's selfless love.

- Our love is shallow with no depth v/s God's love is deep and everlasting.

- Our love has no meaning and functions by emotion v/s God's love that is steadfast and doesn't act on emotion.

- Our love is conditional v/s God's love that is unconditional.

- Our love disengages when the going gets tough v/s God's love empowers us to take His calling.

- Our love runs and hides and withdraws to ourselves v/s God's love that hides us in the shadow of the Almighty.

- Our love brings discouragement in a hopeless situation v/s God's love that gives hope to a dying world.

- Our love causes people to covet and envy materialism v/s God's love that draws people to desire more of Him.

- Our love causes us to run from God v/s God's love that brings us to Him.

- Our love causes perfection v/s God's love that brings reflection of Him.

- Our love allows the pain to remain v/s God's love heals the pain and restores our joy.

Read page 119 in the book *"Touch Me"*.

Maybe you have been in a struggle for many years and it seems like it will never end. Sometimes we not only begin to question ourselves but also God. When God told me that I was selfish believe me it stung to the core of my being. However, I could not begin to get past the selfishness in my soul until I bound a selfish spirit in Jesus' Name and began to thank God that I was no longer selfish. I began to **declare** God's word daily and not just read and meditate on it. In this process God showed me embedded wounds that were covered up by the selfishness in my heart. The redemption that Jesus brought on the cross by shedding His blood was beginning to surface upon the entrenched pain in my heart. Now I was beginning to be shaped on the Potter's wheel of God-centeredness and not self-centeredness.

Refer to the image on page 120 in the book *"Touch Me"*.

I can hear some of you saying, "What does making war in the heavenlies mean?"

"For we are not wrestling with flesh and blood (contending only with physical opponents), but against the despotisms, against the powers, against (the master spirits who are) the world rulers of this present darkness, against the spirit forces of wickedness in the heavenly (supernatural) sphere." (Ephesians 6:12 AMP)

God showed me that I couldn't fight against myself or others. As I began to incline my heart to listen to God and declare His word instead of contending with myself or others, He began a process of revelations that brought transformation to my heart and mind and manifestations of His goodness in my life.

I have included a declaration for our marriage that I wrote from I Corinthians 13 and can be declared for all marriages. As I declared this word God began to not only change and soften my heart but hope began to rise within my heart when some situations looked hopeless and remained unchanged.

Love Walk Hit List

I declare in the name of Jesus that Fred and I have fulfilled God's purpose for loving Him first and then loving each other the way God created us to love.

Therefore, we are patient and kind and endure with each other. We are never envious or jealous of each other's gifts and talents. We do not boast or have any haughtiness in us. We only desire the will of God for our lives and to love each other. Fred and I are not arrogant or inflated with pride when the other one does not understand natural or spiritual revelations. We are not rude with each other but are patient in our communication. We communicate in truth and love. We do not put the others ideas or opinions down but we take them before God for His final word.

Fred and I fill all the needs that God expects us to meet in each other. Fred is my gift from God and I am his gift. We treat each other with joy and excitement and thankfulness for the gift He has given us. We are not self seeking but only seek God for His plan and purpose for our lives. We do not insist on our rights but consider each other's and lay them at the feet of Jesus.

Fred and I are not touchy or fretful or resentful. We continually sit in the Lord's presence for Him to examine our hearts so we do not examine each other. We do not judge or criticize each other therefore; we show mercy because of the mercy given to us from God.

We do not continue on the wrong doings but choose immediately to forgive each other so that God will always forgive us. We hold no record of the past sins since God has wiped our slates clean and we do not live under the enemy's condemnation and guilt. We know that there is no condemnation to those who are in Jesus Christ and called according to His purpose.

We do not rejoice at injustice and unrighteousness, but rejoice when right and truth prevails. When trials and tribulations come into our lives, we do not try to run but embrace the love God has for us that causes us to triumph in victory as we embrace each other. Fred and I believe the best in each other and we continue to bring encouragement that counteracts Satan's poison of discouragement. God's love never fails because we are enflamed in His love.

When we were children we talked, thought and reasoned like a child. Now we are a man and woman in Christ and have done away with our childish ways.

We continue to look into the mirror of God's word and seek His reflection of what God intends us to look like to become more like Jesus. Therefore, I declare in the name of Jesus that we have and will continue until God calls us home, the euphoric love in our marriage that will spill out to many many many marriages!

Read pages 120-121 in the book *"Touch Me"*.

Refer to Jeremiah 33:3 in the book *"Touch Me"*.

I continued to ask God to search my heart and to *reveal* what needed to be changed. He *revealed* a structure that had been erected in my heart to protect myself from being wounded. This caused a barrier between other people that blocked me from receiving God's best in my life. I had been crying out to the Lord for years for the ability to love others with His love yet my own selfish love could not conquer the wounds in my heart.

I was trying to keep my heart safe from being offended. Little did I know that the offenses were the culprit that prevented me from breaking through to God's love. When God gave me this *revelation* I gave Him the offense and received His words of defense that brought a breakthrough in my life.

A brother offended is harder to be won over than a strong city, and (their) contentions separate them like the bars of a castle. (Proverbs 18:19 AMP)

I am reminded of times when I've driven through an underprivileged area of a larger city. Many of the buildings had bars on them to barricade thieves from robbing them during the day or evening. Those bars were made of solid metal which caused a major separation of anyone's attempt to break through.

When we are holding bars of offense from a wrong done to us it not only separates us from others but prevents us from receiving God's love for ourselves and other people.

Perhaps you aren't aware of the bars of offense in your heart and have been settling for second best in your life. Ask the Lord to reveal any offenses that you may not be aware of and lift the bars from your heart. Pray this with me.

Father, I know that I have had wrongs done to me. I thought that I was okay since I didn't get angry at the person or say anything that would displease you. However, I need you to reveal any bars of offense that have been separating me from other people and preventing me from receiving your love for me and others. I bind the spirit of offense and loose your defensive word that frees my heart from being wounded. Your word says that you will perfect that which concerns me and that your mercy and loving kindness endures forever. (Psalm 138:8 AMP) In Jesus' Name. Amen.

Refer to image on pages 121-122 in the book ***"Touch Me"***.

God was teaching me to focus on Him who is the greatest GIFT not on the gifts He could give me.

Is the Holy Spirit saying, "Give me this . . . give me that?"

How long has it been since you have loved God for who He is and not what He can do for you?

God has given us many blessings in this life that many times have been taken for granted. How long has it been since you came to God without your to do list and blessed Him with your praise and worship?

One of the ladies in our church, Lou Ann Shafer, wrote an acronym for each letter of **worship.**

W	*Wonder of Him*
O	*Opening up to Him*
R	*Resting in Him*
S	*Service to Him*
H	*Hearing Him*
I	*Inspired by Him*
P	*Passion for Him*

Refer to the image on page 123 in the book *"Touch Me"*.

How long has it been since you have been blessed by God's presence?

When you come to God with an awe or <u>wonder</u> of Him your heart and mind begin to <u>open up</u> to Him. As your heart and mind are opened you begin to <u>rest</u> in Him which brings freedom from mental and emotional anxiety. When you are resting in the Lord, He gives you the capability of <u>serving</u> Him which brings refreshment in your soul. When you continue to love and serve Him with all of your heart, soul and mind the Holy Spirit's voice becomes more distinct and you <u>hear</u> more of His <u>inspiration</u>. As you continue spending time with God daily you begin to develop intense enthusiasm and <u>passion</u> for Him!

Refer to pages 123-125 in the book *"Touch Me"*.

These pages refer to two special women who came to Jesus in diverse environments for distinct reasons in appointed times yet both fell at His feet and touched His heart.

The sinful woman came to Jesus with a broken and contrite heart for the sin that had plagued her. Mary came because she had a loving relationship with Jesus that brought her to bless Him.

1.   What lessons did Jesus teach us in these two events?

When we sit in the Holy Spirit's classroom daily He teaches us many lessons. I believe Jesus taught the disciples that we are to be like both of these women. There are times when He reveals the sin in our heart that brings us closer to Him with a contrite and humble heart. Other times

as we become more intimate in our relationship with Him we fall to our knees with an overwhelming love for Him.

Refer to the image on page 125 in the book ***"Touch Me"***.

As we look at I John 4:20 we **become aware of** a very strong message from the Lord!

Read pages 126-127 in the book ***"Touch Me"***.

When God made me aware of the **critical** and **judgmental** spirit that had me in its clutches I asked the Lord for His mercy and forgiveness. I want you to understand that I wasn't verbally saying judgmental and critical remarks . . . but thinking them! As long as we continue to entertain these judgmental thoughts about someone we will eventually speak critical words to them.

Until He spoke to me during the night I hadn't been aware that I was entertaining these thoughts that were not only detrimental to my well being but contradicted my love for God.

One day the Lord gave me this vision. I was standing up close to a person speaking critical words. I was so close to the person that there was no room for anyone to be between us. All of a sudden I stepped back and Jesus stepped in front of me.

When we step back from saying critical remarks to others we allow Jesus to step in with his mercy and forgiveness for us and the other person.

We had scheduled a renewal for the ministry. Due to some unforeseen changes we were not able to hold it at the place we had scheduled so we moved the renewal to our home. Since all of the team was able to attend, we had planned to take a group picture of everyone including my husband. It was an unusually hot and humid day for the month of May so my husband decided he would wear shorts for an outdoor picture. I hadn't wanted him to wear shorts but he insisted on wearing them. He had already decided that he would grow a beard that was in the beginning stages of being fully grown which meant that he would look unshaven. My focus was so much on what he was wearing and what he would look like that I wasn't paying attention to what shoes I had on. We had some people that were coming from another area that I had never met. We were in the midst of worship when I happened to look down at my shoes. Would you believe? One shoe was open toe and the other one was closed. I was so embarrassed that I put my one foot behind the other one so they wouldn't notice it. When we took a break for lunch I knew that I had to come clean and let the team know what I did. They were amazed that none of them had noticed it and were really amused. Believe me, normally even if my skirt isn't completely straight one of them will notice it and let me know. My shoes stuck out like a sore thumb in the picture. To top it off Fred was hidden behind me so you couldn't see his shorts and I was in the front row with one open toe and one closed shoe! Needless to say, I felt like crawling into a hole so no one could see me. After I recovered from the embarrassment I shared this lesson with everyone at the renewal. I realized that if I hadn't been focused and critical of what Fred was wearing and had focused on myself I wouldn't have made that mistake. I believe that God knew the lesson that I needed to learn and teach others.

"Don't pick on people, jump on their failures, and criticize their faults unless, of course, you want the same treatment. That critical spirit has a way of boomeranging. It's easy to see a smudge on your neighbor's face and be oblivious to the ugly sneer on your own. Do you have the nerve to say, 'Let me wash your face for you,' when your own face is distorted by contempt? It's this whole traveling road-show mentality all over again, playing a holier-than-thou part instead of just living your part. Wipe that ugly sneer off your own face, and you might be fit to offer a washcloth to your neighbor." (Matthew 7:1-5 Message)

Are you sitting on God's throne of mercy, love and forgiveness looking through His eyes or are you sitting on your judgment seat looking through your eyes? Let's be honest!

Perhaps as you have read this nugget and meditated on the scripture you have felt the conviction of the Holy Spirit and are saying, "Did I do that?" Or perhaps you are saying, "I don't do that!" Oh, really? Are you ready to find out what the Holy Spirit says? If so, please pray this with me.

Father, your word says that we are to remove the beam of timber in our own eye. I bind the negative spirits of judgment and criticism and

loose your mercy and love. Holy Spirit reveal where I have entertained judgmental and critical thoughts in my mind that I have not been aware of. (Please take a moment to hear His voice of revelation.) Please forgive me for judging and criticizing others verbally or in my mind. Thank you for removing the beam from my eyes so that I may see through your eyes and help other people to see you. In Jesus Name. Amen.

Refer to the image on page 127 in the book *"Touch Me".*

Now God has given me another revelation. This process now has a name called the **Hit List!**

In this world there are wicked people who consider problematic people their enemy that need to be dealt with so they hire a hit man to murder them.

In the spiritual world we have an enemy that has every human being on his hit list. Romans 8:31 says, "If God is for us who can be against us?" We are more than conquerors because of Jesus' death and resurrection that conquered satan and his cohorts. So God has given us His word of truth that becomes His **Hit List** against the enemy of our souls.

Read pages 128-130 in the book *"Touch Me".*

As I began to pull out my **Hit List** daily that consisted of binding and loosing, calling things as though they are, confessing God's word over me and others, I began to receive more *revelations*. I began to realize that more changes were taking place within my heart such as:

- The tool of God's word was breaking through my stubborn resistance. (Jeremiah 23:29AMP)

- I was no longer feeling imprisoned in my heart. (refer to image on page 128)

- I began to spend time with the Lord not because of duty but love for Him.

- I knew that God's word was discerning the thoughts and intentions of my heart. (Hebrews 4:12 NKJ)

- My faith was rising and my spirit was connecting with the Holy Spirit.

- I wasn't feeling worried and anxious as I had been in the past.

- I stopped begging God to fit into my plan.

- I began to give the small things to God as well as the big things.

- I was attending more praise services and less pity parties.

- I began to choose to carry God's peace and not give it to the enemy.

One night I had two consecutive dreams with a different outcome. In the first dream two very vicious bears were trying to come after me. I was inside a building feeling very fearful and anxious as I watched them trying to knock the door down. They tried every way they could to get in yet they couldn't succeed. Suddenly they found an opening and crawled through it. I stood frozen in terror as they began to approach me. As they were about to grab me I hastily picked up some food and tossed it to them. After they ate the food they walked out the door.

In the second dream these same bears came in through a similar opening that wasn't as large as the first one. However, I noticed the bears were not as fierce and were calmer which contrasted with the first dream. As they began to approach me I wasn't cowering in fear but knew immediately what to do. Again I picked up more food to feed them, however this time they ate out of my hands. I no longer felt anxious or afraid as peace began to engulf me. Afterwards, they walked out the door.

As I prayed about these dreams, the Holy Spirit showed me that the two bears represented a spirit of fear and anxiety. When I cowered in fear I allowed satan's words to overtake me. Notice in the first dream I tossed the food since I wasn't confident within myself. However, when I began to feed them with

God's word their control over my mind and heart began to lessen and the attacks from the enemy began to cease.

When the spirit of fear and anxiety come knocking on your door pick up the word of God and feed those spirits with His word which brings peace. Each time they come knocking the attacks will lessen and you'll rise up with confidence in God's word!

Refer to the exercise on peace on page 130 in the book ***"Touch Me"***.

Are you carrying God's peace? Place instrumental music in the background and have the leader of the group read this exercise on peace. If you are not in a group setting, place the instrumental music on and read this out loud to yourself.

Read pages 131-133 including the images in the book ***"Touch Me"***.

As I continued the **Hit List** more changes began to take place.

- I began to see God's military forces mounting instead of my problems.

- I began to take all my cases under God's advisement.

Refer to two images on page 133 in the book ***"Touch Me"***.

- Peace was moving in and kicking fear out!

- I received a ***revelation*** of the fear that was rooted within my heart and mind.

- My relationship with God was becoming more cultivated which promoted growth.

Read pages 134-136 in the book ***"Touch Me"***.

- Excitement was welling up in my spirit.

- I stopped chasing the devil and began to chase God who had the devil under his feet.

- I began to not only hear God's **revelations** but began to see in the spirit what had not manifested in my life as yet.

- I stopped limiting God and began to see His power as limitless.

- I began to feel hope rise up and no longer felt the situations were hopeless.

- Unbelief and fear were being replaced by belief and faith.

- I no longer was begging God to change other people but to change me.

- My mind, will and emotions began to change.

Refer to two images on page 136 in the book *"Touch Me"*.

- I became finer tuned in discerning the voice of the Holy Spirit.

- I began to see myself as an over comer rather than overcome by the sin.

- I was no longer talking about my problems but talked to the problem.

- I gave God my victim mentality and began to see the victory!

Refer to the two images on page 137 in the book *"Touch Me"*.

The 1st image says, "The wind of my Holy Spirit will surpass the wind of your circumstances." SO . . . what does this mean?

Let's take a look at the wind of the Holy Spirit's capability!

When the day of Pentecost came, they were all together in one place. Suddenly a sound like the blowing of a violent wind came from heaven and filled the whole house where they were sitting. They saw what seemed to be tongues of fire that separated and came to rest on each of them. All of them were filled with the Holy Spirit and began to speak in other tongues as the Spirit enabled them. (Acts 2:1-4 NIV)

The Greek meaning for spirit and wind is breath. (Strong's)

Remember the Red Sea Miracle! God parted the waters of the sea which enabled the Israelites to cross to the other side on dry land.

Then Moses stretched out his hand over the sea and GOD, with a terrific east wind all night long, made the sea go back. He made the sea dry ground. The seawaters split. (Exodus 14:21 Message)

After all of the Israelites had crossed the Red Sea, God's breath brought the sea back and swallowed up the Egyptians as they sank in the forceful waters.

You (Lord) blew with Your wind, the sea covered them; (clad in mail) they sank as lead in the mighty waters. (Exodus 15:10 AMP)

Circumstances or storms that are beyond our control can blow in suddenly that threaten to devastate us. Let's take a look at the disciples' experience and reaction in their boat.

And a furious storm of wind (of hurricane proportions) arose, and the waves kept beating into the boat, so that it was already becoming filled. But He (Himself) was in the stern (of the boat), asleep on the (leather) cushion; and they awoke Him and said to Him, "Master, do You not care that we are perishing?" (Mark 4:37-38 AMP)

Now we hear Jesus' response to the storm and to the fear in His disciples.

And He arose and rebuked the wind and said to the sea, "Hush now! Be still (muzzled)!" And the wind ceased (sank to rest as if exhausted by its beating) and there was (immediately) a great calm (a perfect peacefulness). He said to them, "Why are you so timid and fearful? How is it that you

have no faith (no firmly relying trust)?" And they feared exceedingly, and said one to another, "What manner of man is this, that even the wind and the sea obey him?" (Mark 4:39-41 AMP)

Jesus taught the disciples and all of us a lesson of what to do when a sudden storm comes up. This was an opportunity for Jesus to show His power and authority over the enemy. As you pray the **Hit List** by taking authority over the circumstances in Jesus' Name and confessing the God—breathed word you will demonstrate to the enemy who you are in the Lord!

Every Scripture is God-breathed (given by His inspiration) and profitable for instruction, for reproof and conviction of sin, for correction of error and discipline in obedience, (and) for training in righteousness (in holy living, in conformity to God's will in thought, purpose, and action) (II Timothy 3:16 AMP)

Now it was time for God's revelations on my negative expectations and thoughts that prevented His ***manifestations***!

2.   List the three steps towards this process of renewal in the mind.

I can hear some of you saying, "How can my negative thoughts be sin?" Or, "I never realized that as I have entertained negative thoughts it was a sin."

When we allow these negative thoughts to remain in our mind we begin to believe what satan says and no longer believe God's word! Our emotions jump on the band wagon along with our negative words. Eventually we lose sight of God's plan and sink into despondency which has been satan's plot all along. Sin separates us from receiving God's love and wreaks havoc in our life.

Let's take a look at what God **feels** when we believe satan's words over His.

God delivered the Israelites from their task master in Egypt and continually proved His faithfulness to the Israelites in the desert. His plan was to bring them **through** the desert experience **knowing** and **trusting** Him in a greater way. He performed miracles to give testimony of His great love for them. The desert was not to be their home. God was leading them into the Promised

Land that was filled with milk and honey. Yet they listened to their negative thoughts in their mind that led to negative words.

But the men who had gone up with him said, "We can't attack those people; they are stronger than we are." And they spread among the Israelites a bad report about the land they had explored. They said, "The land we explored devours those living in it. All the people we saw there are of great size. We saw the Nephilim there (the descendants of Anak come from the Nephilim). We seemed like grasshoppers in our own eyes, and we looked the same to them." (Numbers 13:31-33 NIV)

Notice what the Israelites thought about themselves. They looked at their weaknesses and not the strength God would give them as they trusted Him.

Now we see negative thoughts that brought strong emotions which led to their reactions.

And all the congregation cried out with a loud voice, and (they) wept that night. All the Israelites grumbled and deplored their situation, accusing Moses and Aaron, to whom the whole congregation said, "Would that we had died in Egypt! Or that we had died in this wilderness! Why does the Lord bring us to this land to fall by the sword? Our wives and little ones will be a prey. Is it not better for us to return to Egypt? And they said one to another, Let us choose a captain and return to Egypt." (Numbers 14:1-4 AMP)

Now let's hear God's response in all of this grumbling.

And the Lord said to Moses and Aaron, "How long will this evil congregation murmur against Me? I have heard the complaints the Israelites murmur against Me."

Tell them, As I live, says the Lord, what you have said in My hearing I will do to you: **Your dead bodies shall fall in this wilderness—of all who were numbered of you, from twenty years old and upward, who have murmured against Me. (Numbers 14:26-30 AMP)**

Did you catch this? The Israelites not only allowed the negativity in their mind and heart but sealed their own fate by their words!

Let's compare the Apostle Paul's response to the negativity in his mind v/s the Israelites' response.

So I find this law at work: Although I want to do good, evil is right there with me. For in my inner being I delight in God's law; but I see another law at work in me, waging war against the law of my mind and making me a prisoner of the law of sin at work within me. What a wretched man I am! Who will rescue me from this body that is subject to death? Thanks be to God, who delivers me through Jesus Christ our Lord! So then, I myself in my *mind* am a slave to God's law, but in my sinful nature a slave to the law of sin. (Romans 7:21-25 NIV)

Paul saw the battle of his flesh v/s the Holy Spirit. He believed God's word over the enemy of his soul.

But He said to me, "My grace (My favor and loving-kindness and mercy) is enough for you (sufficient against any danger and enables you to bear the trouble manfully); for My strength and power are made perfect (fulfilled and completed) and show themselves most effective in (your) weakness." Therefore, I will all the more gladly glory in my weaknesses and infirmities, that the strength and power of Christ (the Messiah) may rest (yes, may pitch a tent over and dwell) upon me! So for the sake of Christ, I am well pleased and take pleasure in infirmities, insults, hardships, persecutions, perplexities and distresses; for when I am weak (in human strength), then am I (truly) strong (able, powerful in divine strength). (II Corinthians 12:9-10 AMP))

I can do all this through him who gives me strength. (Philippians 4:13 NIV)

So are you looking at your weaknesses or God's strength in your weaknesses?

Refer to image on page 138 in the book *"Touch Me"*.

3.   What five things did God speak to me about my mind?

Read pages 138-139 in the book ***"Touch Me"***.

4. When our emotions waver what happens to us?

5. When are we fair game for the devil?

Are you in a situation that has caused you to be like a scared rabbit hiding behind a tree? (Refer to the image on page 139 in the book ***"Touch Me".)***

6. What is satan's objective for God's children?

7. What is God's objective for His children?

8. Overcoming the negative thoughts by confessing God's word is the beginning of what process?

9. When we continually entertain the negativity in our minds who has the victory?

10. How do we create a diversion of the negativity in our minds?

11. What takes place in that diversion?

Refer to the image on page 140 in the book ***"Touch Me".***

Many times we don't realize what we are saying because we have been so accustomed to saying it. One day the Holy Spirit spoke to me about familiar spirits. They are called familiar because they have been so common to us that we haven't recognized what damage they are creating in our life. When the Holy Spirit spoke this word to me I began to ask Him to show me what I have not recognized that has been familiar.

Let me give you an example of what took place in my mind recently. I have always had a problem even as a child with cold weather and would actually dread the winter season in Pennsylvania. One evening I experienced my body feeling as though it were chilled to the bone. I could hardly function in my mind inside our home let alone think about going outside in the cold weather. I even took my temperature thinking I might have a fever. As I was sitting on our sofa all bundled up in blankets, I heard the Holy Spirit say, "Thank me for winter. You will have opportunities in the winter that you won't have in the summer." I began to thank Him for winter and for the coming opportunities. Suddenly I felt the Holy Spirit's presence and knew He had broken the stronghold in my mind. I began to thank Him for everything that I could think of at that moment especially for liberation on my mind and heart. The next day it was as though winter didn't exist. Even though the temperature had dropped and was much colder, I no longer felt laden down with my negative thoughts. Two weeks later I had an opportunity to speak at a church basketball game that was reaching out to the community. It's been over two months now and we are still in the winter season. However, I'm not bound in negative winter thoughts any longer! Actually, I can look outside at the snow falling and enjoy God's beautiful wonderland. What a faithful God!

Ask the Lord what familiar spirit as been creating havoc in your life that you have not recognized.

Read and meditate on the scriptures and prayers on thoughts on pages 140-142 in the book ***"Touch Me"***.

Read page 143 along with the image in the book ***"Touch Me"***.

As I continued the **Hit List** the following *manifestations* began to take place.

- I began to see God's heart for me.

- I was focused on God's love not my circumstances.

- I received comfort from confessing God's word.

- My heart was entangled in God's heart.

- I began to leap for joy in the midst of sorrows.

- My heart began to sing when the heaviness was still around me.

- I began to place other's desires above my own.

- I saw the sunshine in the midst of the clouds in my life.

- I began to laugh when I felt like crying.

- I knew that everything was in God's hands.

- My mind was being trained to find something good.

- I was finding peace, joy, forgiveness, love, goodness, meekness, gentleness, kindness and self control.

- My faith was connecting with God's heart for me and my family.

Read I Thessalonians 5:16-18 in the book *"Touch Me"*.

This scripture says that we have a part in this life along with God. In the sport of professional wrestling there is a group of players teamed together to prevail against the opposing team. One from each team is chosen to wrestle against one another for a certain amount of time. The wrestlers change places on each team only after the one who has just wrestled touches the next wrestler on his team. This is what takes place with us and God. As we wrestle with the powers of darkness by making war in the heavenlies with the **Hit List** God does His part in revealing the next step. This tag teaming will continue in our Christian life until the victory is won when we go to our eternal home in heaven.

Are you tag teaming with God or expecting God to do all the work?

As I continued the **Hit List** there were more strongholds in my mind that were being broken. From these visions I have received new pictures on the canvas of my mind when the thoughts try to return.

- I began to realize that God's arm wasn't too short to reach the door of His opportunities. (Refer to the image on page 143 in the book *"Touch Me"*.)

- God wants to show Himself strong through us. (Refer to the image on page 144 in the book *"Touch Me".)*

- It's never hopeless for someone to receive salvation even when they are in dementia. (Refer to the image on page 145 and 146 in the book *"Touch Me".)*

- As we lift up our hands in worship Jesus stops what He is doing, takes time to listen and touches us with His presence. (Refer to the image on page 146 in the book *"Touch Me"*.)

Are you hungry for more of His presence?

As we have come to the last page of this chapter, are you ready to write a hit list? If so, I have included a list of weaknesses that can bring in the enemy's power to control us. I'm going to ask you to take a piece of paper and list two columns as I have shown you on page 118 in the book *"Touch Me"*. Ask the Lord to reveal the weaknesses in your life and family. This will be your homework since it would be too difficult to work on during your classroom study. However, some of you may decide to share it with each other. This list will continue as the Lord reveals those weaknesses in your journey to a more intimate relationship with Him!

Hit List

Confusion vs. clarity of God's word
Pride vs. humility
Deception vs. truth
Attention for ourselves vs. focus on God
Gossip that wounds others vs. kind and loving remarks
Competing for our self worth vs. our worth comes from God
Unforgiveness vs. forgiveness
Childish behavior vs. child-like faith in God
Oppression vs. knowing God's love for us
Criticism vs. praise to God and for others
Manipulation v/s allowing God's control
Judgment vs. mercy
Passiveness vs. active relationship with God

Addictions vs. self control and devotion to God

Poverty vs. lacking none of God's riches

Spiritual jealousy vs. knowledge of who we are in the Lord

Religious spirit vs. intimate relationship with the Lord

Rebellion vs. yielding to God's plan and purpose for your life

Discouragement vs. encouragement

Spiritual blindness vs. God's perspective on self and others

Spiritual deafness vs. hearing God's voice

Distraction vs. intense attraction to God

Torment vs. pleasure with the Lord

Anger vs. peace of God

Immaturity vs. maturity in the Lord

Idolatry vs. adoration and admiration shown to God

Double mindedness vs. decision to follow Christ no matter what

Gluttony vs. behavior that is socially and morally acceptable for your health and well being spiritually and physically.

Laziness vs. energetic physically and spiritually

Intimidation vs. adequacy in the Lord

Offenses vs. God's defensive word against the offense of others

Fear vs. faith in God

Rejection vs. God's acceptance of us

Doubt and unbelief vs. trust in God

Worry and anxiety vs. peace

Bondage vs. freedom

Heaviness vs. lightheartedness and joy of the Lord

Defiant vs. cooperation with God

Antichrist vs. spirit of Christ

Disrespect vs. spirit of respect

Unteachable vs. teachable spirit

Ungrateful vs. thankful spirit

Infirmity vs. God's healing power that frees us from sickness and disease

Self Righteousness vs. righteousness of God

Insensitivity vs. sensitive to the Holy Spirit

Vindictive vs. speaking the truth in love

Abusive vs. self control

Mean spirited vs. spirit of love

Wavering spirit vs. right, persevering and steadfast spirit

Perverted spirit vs. no longer opposing what God's word says is right

Lust vs. feeding the spirit not the flesh

Frustration vs. resting in the Lord

Stubborn spirit vs. non resistant to God's will

Self centered vs. God centered

Cursing spirit vs. blessing God and others

Accusing spirit vs. seeking God for His wisdom of what to say to others

Spirit of disconnection emotionally and spiritually vs. intimacy with God and others

As you spend time in His presence you will receive God's love that will enable you to resist the words of the enemy and give you the capability to be non resistant to God's word.

Tapestry

We may have come to the last chapter in this book but rest assured God will never stop teaching us His lessons as long as we keep our heart and mind opened to hear from Him daily! I believe the older I become and the longer I walk with God the less I know. Just when I think I may have the process for praying for others and myself, God does something I least expect!

Read pages 148-149 in the book *"Touch Me"*.

One day I had this vision when I was praying with someone. I saw a mother and daughter sitting in chairs that were back to back. They were bound with ropes that were holding their arms down preventing them from getting off their chairs. The Holy Spirit revealed a spirit of unforgiveness that was a stronghold keeping them from having a loving relationship. As I prayed with the mother we bound the unforgiving spirit and loosed the spirit of forgiveness. While we were praying suddenly I saw a vision of the ropes being broken around them which brought freedom to love each other. About two weeks later the daughter began to express some pent up emotions to her mother. As the mother listened to the daughter, the daughter chose to forgive and their relationship was no longer strained. In the midst of this the daughter had become very ill with an inflammation in her muscles which eventually brought a diagnosis of cancer. In the next year or so the daughter went through a series of events that included an operation and chemotherapy for many months. In those months she kept seeking God for His wisdom. One night she was dozing on a chair waking up at intervals watching a worship channel. This particular night she woke up to see this scripture on the television screen.

I will not die but live, and will proclaim what the Lord has done. (Psalm 118:17 NIV)

She felt excitement welling up within her spirit and felt this was a word from the Lord for her physical healing and embraced it. In her time of illness she never once believed that she would die. She seized God's word that produced bull dog faith and confessed the healing scriptures daily. One week before her death they called in hospice. The pain had worsened and she needed much stronger medication.

She had such a strong will to live that she wouldn't allow herself to lie down and go to sleep under the medication. She continued to stand up into the late night hours and tell God, "You promised that I would live and not die." Her mother had phoned me from her daughter's home and had me listen to her daughter crying out. It was so heart wrenching that I wanted to take her in my arms to bring her comfort. Afterwards, her cries continued to resonate in my spirit. We all waited with great expectation for the Lord to intervene in the medication and completely heal her body. Surely, God would heal her. After all, she was only forty-five and had two children ages nine and fourteen. How could God's plan for her life be accomplished here on earth when she was a wife and mother and was needed by her husband and children? And what about her mother who had already lost her son about twenty years ago? Hasn't she suffered enough, Lord?

Read the first paragraph on page 150 in the book ***"Touch Me"***.

For weeks I kept feeling that something was missing but didn't know what it was. As I was seeking God to reveal this I received this vision. I saw a puzzle on a table that had a large piece missing in the middle. Jesus was standing beside the table with the piece in His hand.

One week later the daughter went home to be with the Lord. Now we were all left behind with many questions in our mind. Actually, this experience shot down all of the theories on not getting healed because of unbelief. Our team of women confessed the healing scriptures and stood on healing for this daughter daily. In this process of praying and confessing the word we drew even closer to God and our hearts knitted with each other. Our faith was strengthened as we reached out with God's love to her. Our spirits connected with God's spirit and our hearts connected with His heart for her. We hardly knew her yet we felt love for her as though she was our best friend.

Now it was our choice! Were we going to be bitter over this and throw out all of God's word on healing or were we going to recognize that Jesus had the missing piece and He didn't feel any need to check in with us? Years ago as a little child I was always taught that you never question God. After all, He knows what He is doing. Now that I know God won't get upset with me I ask Him questions that I don't understand.

I come to Him not just as a little child in an adult body but as God's child who knows that my Daddy loves and delights in me and is not ready to hit me over the head when I ask Him questions. Even though I don't always receive the answers to my questions, I receive God's love. After the funeral I kept asking God to help me to understand her death. Now don't get me wrong! I know that she is in heaven and is celebrating with the angels and our God! I also know that there is an appointed time for all of us to die. But why did you take her home now? After all, we prayed, confessed and believed for her healing and agreed with your word for her. About a week after the funeral I was in the process of cleaning our house. I heard the Holy Spirit ask me this question. "You don't agree with my decision, do you?" My thought was "Lord, I never said that!" He said, "No, but you have thought it." Then He said, "Now talk to me." I began to weep and tell Him I didn't agree with His decision even though I knew it was His decision to make. I repented of the thoughts and the anger that I felt. Suddenly I felt a new wave of His love and healing power surging through my spirit. You see, God knew what was blocking me from receiving His love and He no longer wanted a barrier between us. I hadn't even realized there was a blockage since I thought I was just mourning.

Now, I'd like to share another situation that took place the same night I received a phone call from the mother. My daughter works in a nursing home. She called to ask me to pray for a woman in her nineties who was really suffering. She wanted me to pray that God would take her home and out of her suffering. I simply prayed this, "Lord, if it's not her time, heal her body but if it's time to take her home please take her home quickly!" That was all I prayed. The next day I received a phone call from my daughter. She said, "Mom, God brought this woman out of all her pain and healed her. They don't know what happened to her since they thought surely she would die." The other day I asked my daughter how this woman is doing. She said that she is no longer in pain and her whole attitude has changed.

God showed me that I had placed my trust in the process of healing and not in God's unfailing love!

But I am like an olive tree flourishing in the house of God; I trust in God's unfailing love forever and ever. (Psalm 52:8 NIV)

I can hear some of you saying, "How will you and the Promise Land Ministries team pray the next time?" We will pray, believe and confess the word that unites our hearts and spirits with God and each other. We will continue to ask the Lord to search our hearts and touch us with His healing power so we can prosper in our hearts and minds. (III John1:2 KJV) We will continue to seek God for a more intimate relationship with Him and ask Him for His wisdom in all situations. Will we be disappointed if our prayer isn't answered for healing? Yes, I believe we will. However, everything we experience in this life will either make us bitter or better. We must make that choice to be better not allowing bitterness to set in our heart. When we become honest with God, ourselves and each other a healing process begins and we truly begin to accept God's unfailing love for us!

The following are the synonyms for unfailing. I encourage you to speak this out loud every day.

- God's love is consistent.

- God's love is dependable.

- God's love is trustworthy.

- God's love is reliable.

- God's love is constant.

- God's love is abiding.

- God's love is lasting.

Maybe you have lost a loved one and prayed, believed and confessed the word yet God chose to take them home. Has God healed you of this pain or are you still carrying the pain of their loss? Have you gotten gut honest with the Lord? We as Christians don't like to admit that we are disappointed with God's decisions. However, as long as we hold these words in our thoughts we place a barrier between us and God and no longer are able to receive His love for us. May I encourage you to get gut honest with yourself, God and others today?

Read page 150 in the book *"Touch Me".*

Read and Meditate on Matthew 11:28-29 on page 150 in the book *"Touch Me".*

I love this scripture since I envision a scene with Jesus and me. I see Him sitting by a quiet stream waiting for me to come to Him.

I feel His pain as He watches me stoop shouldered and dragging my feet while carrying burdens that I wasn't meant to carry. He sees the tiredness in my soul since the load is too much for me to bear. His desire is to free me yet His hands are tied until I come to Him. So every day He comes to the stream ready to offer me refreshment for my soul. I continue to carry not only my burdens but now have become a burden bearer of others. He reaches out to me every day and says, "Come, my child. Give your burdens to me. This is too much for you to bear!" He sees my stiff upper lip that is determined to work out my own problems. He watches as I push myself daily to break through the traffic in my life. I continue to bear these burdens alone until one day I am so discouraged that I can hardly get out of bed. Finally, I cry out to Jesus. "Jesus where are you? I can't carry these burdens any longer. Help me!" Jesus hears my cry and says, "My child, I've been waiting for you to give those burdens to me. Come and sit on my lap. Rest with me." As I crawl up into His lap and begin to rest with Him I feel His arms of comfort. The problems and situations in my life begin to seem smaller as Jesus wraps His strong loving arms around me. I no longer feel the heaviness of the perplexities of life but feel like a weight is being lifted from my mind. As I continue to sit on Jesus lap I begin to drink of His living water and feel the refreshment in my dry parched soul. Now I no longer feel discouragement but have received His encouragement. Because I have been with Jesus and have given Him the burdens I now can rest knowing that He has everything under control. Now I can face the day with a new found trust in Jesus.

How long has it been since you have received His refreshment? I encourage you to picture Jesus in a place where you feel safe, comforted and peaceful. He is waiting for you.

In the morning you hear my voice, O Lord; in the morning I prepare (a prayer, a sacrifice) for you and watch and wait (for you to speak to my heart). (Psalm 5:3 AMP)

I needed the quiet

I needed the quiet so He drew me aside into the shadows where we could confide. Away from the bustle where all the daylong I hurried and worried when active and strong.

I needed the quiet though at first I rebelled but gently, so gently my cross He upheld. He whispered so sweetly of spiritual things, though weakened in body, my spirit took wings to heights never dreamed of when active and gay. He loved me so greatly, He drew me away.

I needed the quiet. No prison my bed, but a beautiful valley of blessings instead and a place to grow richer in Jesus to hide. I needed the quiet so He drew me aside. (Alice Mortenson)

He will feed his flock like a shepherd. He will gather the lambs in His arm. He will carry them in His bosom and will gently lead those that have their young. (Isaiah 40:11 AMP)

He will gather the lambs in His arm . . . this is a description of the Father's love for us!

One day I had a vision of Jesus holding a lamb in His arm. The lamb was so beaten up that it couldn't lift its head. I saw bruises all over the lamb's body. The little lamb could not run and jump with the other lambs since its spirit wasn't free and its little body was quivering. I said, "What does this lamb represent?" The Holy Spirit spoke this to me. "You are this crushed lamb." One year later during this healing process, God gave me another vision. I saw Jesus holding a lamb that was healed. He told me to thank Him for my healing.

The Hebrew word for **crushed** is ***kathath*** (kaw-thah) which means to bruise or strike violently, beat (down to pieces) break in pieces, destroy, smite. (Strong's)

Many of you are crushed lambs. God's word for you today is to thank Him that you are no longer crushed but now are healed lambs. Allow God to hold you in His arms and place His healing in your body, soul and spirit.

One day in my quiet time with the Lord I began to write this to Him and reflect on His love for me.

You are my Shepherd

You are my Shepherd who puts me on the right path.
You are my Shepherd who guides me and lights my path.
You are my Shepherd who protects me from the evil in this world.
You are my Shepherd who gently takes my hand and says, "Have no fear, I have you in my arms.
You are my Shepherd who lovingly picks me up when and I fall and brushes the dirt off me.
You are my Shepherd . . . when I get out of line you gently put me back into place with you.
You are my Shepherd . . . when danger is ahead you go before me and guard me from my enemy.
You are my Shepherd . . . I have no needs for you supply all my needs.
You are my Shepherd who is my rear guard that keeps me from going back to where I was.
You are my Shepherd who carries me when I am too tired and weary to walk.
You are my Shepherd who sees my heart and shines your light on the darkness so I can lay my weaknesses at your feet.
You are my Shepherd who forgives my sins and says, "Go and sin no more."
You are my Shepherd in whom I can run to in the midst of the storm.
You are my Shepherd who calms the waves so I can walk to you.
You are my Shepherd who places others in my path to help me along this journey of life.
You are my Shepherd who shields and protects me.

You are my Shepherd who leads me from the lies of the enemy into your truth.

You are my Shepherd who doesn't judge and condemn me but gives me mercy when I don't deserve it.

You are my Shepherd who says, "It is I . . . don't be afraid."

You are my Shepherd who flashes destruction on the strongholds of my life.

You are my Shepherd who feeds my spirit and gives me your living water when I am hungry and thirst for you.

You are my Shepherd who hears my cry for help and comes running to rescue me from my pain and suffering.

You are my Shepherd who shed your blood and gave your life so I could live with you.

You are my Shepherd who is always on twenty four hour call and there is never call waiting.

You are my Shepherd who heals me when I am sick emotionally, physically, and spiritually.

You are my Shepherd who binds up all of my wounds.

And most of all, you are my Shepherd who loves me without any conditions on my loving you in return.

Do you know this Shepherd? Do you see Jesus as your Shepherd?

So do not fear for I am with you, do not be dismayed for I am your God. I will strengthen you and help you. I will uphold you with my righteous right hand. All who rage against you will surely be ashamed and disgraced. Those who oppose you will be as nothing and perish. (Isaiah 41:10-11 NIV)

Read pages 151 to the second paragraph on page 153 in the book *"Touch Me"*.

Do you see yourself as a couple with God or are you still single?

When we take on God's service He provides the platform and stands beside us imparting His wisdom and inspiration through us to others.

For I (Myself) will give you a mouth and such utterance and wisdom that all of your foes combined will be unable to stand against or refute. (Luke 21:15 AMP)

When a couple is in love they miss their time with each other and can't wait to be in each other's arms. That's the way our relationship should be with God.

I am reminded of how years ago I would go steady with boyfriends. They would buy me an identification bracelet that would have their name on it and that would clinch our relationship. And believe me . . . I showed the bracelet off to all the girls. They knew he was my man and they had better not trespass on my territory.

That's how God feels about us. He has our name engraved on His hands and has given notice to satan that we are God's property!

Behold, I have indelibly imprinted (tattooed a picture of) you on the palm of each of My hands; (O Zion) your walls are continually before Me. (Isaiah 49:16 AMP)

In other words God has permanently written your name on each palm of His hands and you are on His mind constantly.

Think about your very first love in your life. How did you feel? You didn't want anything in your life that would hinder your relationship with them. No matter what decisions you made you always kept them in your heart. When you weren't with them you couldn't wait to be together again.

When you got together with other friends all you could talk about was your love relationship. You couldn't wait to whisper sweetness to them and hear their sweet words in response. No matter what your schedule was like you planned your days around them. Sometimes you sat together in silence watching television and didn't watch what they didn't consent to. You planned your activities together with great delight in each other. You rejoiced in doing small things for them and couldn't wait to see their expressions. There were things that you talked about and placed your confidence in them knowing they wouldn't disclose what you said. Think about the hours that you spent time getting ready for them. Remember those times that you laughed and cried together? Most of all, your main goal in life was to please them because you loved them so much.

This is how we should be treating our God. He should be the lover of your soul. Are you trying to please God because it's your duty or do you please Him because you are in love with Him?

Lately, I've had many phone calls from women who have become desperate for change in their lives. These are some questions that I have asked them and are now encouraging you ponder.

When is the last time you spent **talking** and **listening** to God? Many of us talk to God daily however we don't wait for God to talk with us.

One day the Lord spoke this into my heart. "My children are looking for love in all the places that do not satisfy which causes them to desire more. When my children look to me I bring satisfaction and fulfillment into their heart."

All of us have an innate longing to be loved! However, many people are looking for love in all the wrong places to fill the void of love and acceptance which leads to seeking popularity, fame, self-promotion, wealth, or falling into addictions of alcohol, drugs, sex, cutting, bulimia or anorexia! As we look around us we see misconceptions of love portrayed on the television, internet and through many songs.

Where are you looking for love to fill that void in your heart?

The following is a letter that was written by a student who had an addiction:

Just One More Time

The starving sensation of hot chemical lurking within me and the constant struggle it brings killing me every time I give in. The way it makes me feel so good inside, but is destroying not only me but everyone I love. The way I promise that I will never give in again, but somehow it has me back into its arms by nightfall. It makes me justify things that I never thought I would do

167

and makes promises to me that I want to believe, but are nothing but deceit. It has a hold of me now, I no longer have control . . . . it controls me.

It screams at me saying "You need me, just one more time." It plays with me. I am nothing but another lost soul that it has destroyed. It laughs at me saying, "You chose to take me in and you believed in me."

A man relayed an experience he had encountered. He had a **stronghold** in his mind from wounds in his heart that produced an **addiction.** As a young teen he had a desire to see the power of satan and actually asked for it. Satan heard this young teen's words and came on the scene with the **enticement** of drugs. He **seduced** him with a high that he had never experienced. He yielded to satan's **temptation** and has continued to **justify** his actions into his forties. One day instead of telling the truth of why he wasn't coming home on time he decided to speak satan's words of **deception** to his family. It was raining outside and since he had drugs and alcohol in his system, He decided to go walking on a path that he had never been to sober up! For a while he was enjoying the scenery that included deer and other wildlife. However, due to his unwariness he unexpectedly walked into many snags that began to hinder his steps. As he continued on the path he became entangled in some brushes. Suddenly he realized that he had not been paying attention to the path that led him back to the road and didn't know his way out!

One day as I was telling the Lord how much I loved Him. He spoke this into my spirit. "You love me but you don't realize the depth of my love for you. Take my hand, Jenny and I will take you on this journey of love!"

That Christ may dwell in your hearts through faith that you being rooted and grounded in love may be able to comprehend with all the saints what is the width and length and depth and height to know the love of Christ which passes knowledge that you may be filled with all the fullness of God. (Ephesians 3:17-19 NKJ)

Are you on a journey seeking more of God's love or have you been seduced into satan's trap of deception and fallen into the pit of addictions?

So . . . what is keeping you from being a couple with God?

Perhaps it is . . . bitterness!

If so, this is God's encouragement and healing for you from His word.

My child, give me the bitterness in your soul. You have me inside therefore; you have my love for you and for others. Love me with all of your heart, soul and mind and you will be able to draw from my well of love within you. Let me heal this deep, deep pain within you. Come tell me where it hurts! Come to me. Now . . . receive all of my love for you.

Do you doubt God's word?

My child, give me the doubt in your heart. Embrace the life I have for you and nothing will be too much. Tell this mountain in your life to go jump in the lake and it's as good as done. Talk to me about everything whether it's small or large in your eyes. Continue to give me the pain of loss! Embrace Me! Trust Me! Come to me. Now receive everything I have for you today. (Mark 11:24 Message)

Are you allowing fear to control your life?

My child, give me all of your fear. When you listen to my words, I give you faith to believe. When you listen and speak negative words, you believe the enemies words over mine. Do not be seized with alarm and struck with fear. Evil can't get close to you; harm can't get through the door. I have ordered my angels to guard you wherever you go. If you stumble, they'll catch you; their job is to keep you from falling. You'll walk unharmed among lions and snakes and kick young lions and serpents from the path. Come to me. Hold onto me . . . Now receive my faith for all your situations today! (Luke 12:32 AMP, Psalm 91 Message)

Do you have a hot temper?

My child, give me this temper. I have watched you all throughout your years and I see how you have been rejected. I have called you to bridle the anger, trash your wrath and cool your pipes. It only makes things worse! Come lay your head on my lap. Let me put my arms around you. Come to

me. When you receive my forgiveness you will be able to forgive others as I have forgiven you today! (Psalm 37:8 Message)

Are you filled with anxiety?

My child, I have watched you for many years and see the burdens that you carry. I have cried for you and with you. You try to be so brave and hold the pain inside. My desire is to free you. Lay your burdens at my feet today. I have not called you to worry or be anxious about anything in this life. I am in control. I am the God of the Angel armies and own all the silver and gold. I am living and breathing among you right now. There is nothing too difficult for me. Don't look at what may or may not happen tomorrow. I will help you deal with whatever hard things come up when the time comes. Come to me. Now . . . receive my peace like a transcending river that flows on and on for all of your situations today! (Haggai 2:5, 8, Philippians 4:7)

He is calling you to come to Him. He is not just a God of love . . . He is love!

The following scriptures are taken from the word LOVE!

L . . . . Is He the lover of your soul? Jesus replied, "Love the Lord your God with all your heart and with all your soul and with all your mind." (Matthew 22:37 NIV)

O . . . . Is your faith an over comer? "For whatever is born of God overcomes the world; and this is the victory that has overcome the world, our faith." (I John 5:4 NKJ)

V . . . . Is God your vine? "I am the vine; you are the branches. Whoever lives in Me and I in him bears much (abundant) fruit. However, apart from Me (cut off from vital union with Me) you can do nothing." (John 15:5 AMP)

E . . . . Are your eyes of understanding enlightened? "I do not cease to give thanks for you, making mention of you in my prayers that the God of our Lord Jesus Christ, the Father of glory, may give to you the spirit of wisdom and revelation in the knowledge of Him, the eyes of your understanding being enlightened; that you may know what is the hope of His calling, what are the riches of the glory of His inheritance in the saints." (Ephesians 1:16-18 NKJ)

Are you desperate to be with Him?

Some of you may be saying "But I have had this stronghold in my life for many years. I have even been through rehab and thought I was delivered but found that I wasn't. I am on the same path of destruction and can't find my way out!"

You are not alone! Jesus wants to remove what no one can touch in you. Come with expectation and thank Him for your deliverance in your heart and mind.

A desperate prayer opens the gates of heaven. There is no limit to what God will do when you believe His word. He has an unlimited supply for all your needs in every area of your life when you don't limit Him. Will you come boldly to His throne room and receive what He has stored up for you? Will you wear His identification bracelet and couple with Him? If so, pray this with me.

Lord, I am so desperate for you to show me the way out of this stronghold. I have tried so many other ways and nothing has worked. I am sorry this addiction (name it) has taken control of my life and I ask that you forgive me for yielding to this temptation. I ask you to take control on my heart and mind. I ask you to examine my heart and mind and reveal what areas need to be healed to set me free of this addiction. Your Word says that you are the vine and I am the branch. When I live in you and you in me I will bear abundant fruit. I have been cut off from union with you by my own stubborn will. Therefore, I bind the spirit of addiction and loose self-control on every area of my life. I break satan's power over me and thank you for your deliverance! In Jesus' Name. Amen.

My soul yearns, yes, even pines and is homesick for the courts of the Lord; my heart and my flesh cry out and sing for joy to the living God. (Psalm 84:2 AMP)

Jenny Hagemeyer

Refer to the images on page 153 in the book *"Touch Me"*.

I was visiting my mother for a couple of days. One of her friends had gone home to be with the Lord. We decided to attend the funeral that was in the church where I had grown up and was married for the first time. I saw people that I hadn't seen for over forty years. Many happy and sad memories surged through my mind as we talked with each one of them. It was as though there was a special memory card that was placed into the camera of my mind and suddenly all the pictures surfaced. Another day I visited a friend that I hadn't seen for over twenty years. Again another memory card was placed in the camera of my mind and we laughed and reminisced over the past. Another day was a visit with one of my neighbors where I had lived when I met Fred. We had the closeness of sisters and even went on vacations together. Again another memory card was placed in the camera of our minds and we laughed and cried with each other.

When I returned home I realized that I had been met with a blast from my past. I saw in every segment of my life how God has been weaving a common thread of joys and sorrows. I began to see my life like a patchwork quilt and saw Jesus lovingly and painstakingly taking all my experiences, perplexities, loving and unloving people, and surroundings from my past weaving them into my future that was bringing me closer to His plan and purpose for my life. Every gap in the patches of my life was being closed and every pain and sorrow was being stitched by His healing hand. He was interlacing all my sorrows and joys of the past with His love, mercy, forgiveness and grace. My past, present and future were being intertwined with His perfect love.

Many people hold God responsible for evil acts that take place in this world but He is never liable for evil. However, God weaves all of our experiences and circumstances in life together to create His divine tapestry transporting us into a realm of faith in God's sovereignty which helps us to embrace His deep love for us!

The Lord will keep you from all evil; He will keep your life. The Lord will keep your going out and your coming in from this time forth and forevermore. (Psalm 121:7-8 AMP)

The Lord will perfect that which concerns me. Your mercy and loving-kindness, O Lord, endure forever. Forsake not the works of your own hands. (Psalm 138:8 AMP)

Read pages 154-155 in the book *"Touch Me"*.

Jesus eventually chose twelve disciples, however we are going to take a look at two of his disciples Simon Peter and his brother Andrew.

Let's take a look behind the scenes that led Andrew and Peter to have an encounter with Jesus. Peter was a fisherman for many years at Bethsaida, a name meaning house of fish. Afterwards, he resided in Capernaum where Jesus frequently spent time in His ministry. His brother Andrew was also a fisherman. As little boys they probably watched their father, Jonah as he took fish to the market to be sold to feed his family. I can imagine these little boys saying, "When I grow up I want to be a fisherman just like my daddy."

Andrew and Simon Peter became a disciple of John the Baptist before becoming a disciple of Jesus.

The next day John was there again with two of his disciples. When he saw Jesus passing by, he said, "Look, the Lamb of God!" When the two disciples heard him say this, they followed Jesus. Turning around, Jesus saw them following and asked, "What do you want?" They said, "Rabbi" (which means "Teacher"), "where are you staying?" "Come," he replied, "and you will see." So they went and saw where he was staying, and they spent that day with him. It was about four in the afternoon. Andrew, Simon Peter's brother, was one of the two who heard what John had said and who had followed Jesus. (John 1:35-40 NIV)

Can you imagine the excitement in Andrews's spirit as he spends time sitting at Jesus feet listening to His teaching? I'm sure that many thoughts were on his mind. Did he think, "I can't wait to tell Peter where I was today?" Wow! I never want this day to end." Did he feel like he had to pinch himself? After all, he was in the presence of the Messiah.

Andrew is known as the first missionary that led someone to Christ since he introduced his brother Peter to Jesus.

He first sought out and found his own brother Simon and said to him, "We have found (discovered) the Messiah!—which translated is the Christ (the Anointed One)." Andrew then led (brought) Simon to Jesus. Jesus looked at him and said, "You are Simon son of John. You shall be called Cephas—which translated is Peter (Stone)." (John 1:41-42 AMP)

After the encounter with Jesus, Peter and Andrew continued every day with their business of fishing until one day the divine power of Jesus called them to **give up their will and pick up God's plan** by following Him!

As He was walking by the Sea of Galilee, He noticed two brothers, Simon who is called Peter and Andrew his brother, throwing a dragnet into the sea, for they were fishermen. And He said to them, "Come after Me (as disciples—letting Me be your Guide), follow Me, and I will make you fishers of men!" At once they left their nets and became His disciples (sided with His party and followed Him). (Matthew 4:18-20 AMP)

His divine power has given us everything we need for a godly life through our knowledge of him who called us by his own glory and goodness. Through these he has given us his very great and precious promises, so that through them you may participate in the divine nature, having escaped the corruption in the world caused by evil desires. (II Peter 1:3-4 NIV)

From this day forward their life was never going to be the same. They had been fishermen of the sea and now Jesus was changing their profession to the ministry of being fishers of men and women. Had they counted the cost? There is no record of Peter and Andrew asking Jesus any questions before they were chosen to be His disciples. The Bible says, **at once** they left their nets and became His disciples. They didn't hesitate or say "Let us think about it?"

I thought about questions they could have pondered in their heart in counting the cost of following Jesus.

Did they have any clue from their first meeting with Jesus that they would be chosen to be His disciple? Would they be willing to surrender their life for Jesus when the going gets tough? Could they leave their friends and family behind to follow Him? Would they miss all the times of bringing in a huge catch of fish while feeling the pride in bringing in a vast income from their business?

Would they go into dangerous places and cower in fear? Were they strong enough to walk with Jesus or would they become tired and feel like giving up? Would they be willing to sit at Jesus' feet and learn things that they had never seen or heard?

The word disciple is taken from a Greek word that means learner. (Strong's)

Did they know they were born to serve the purpose of God?

A man's heart plans his way but the Lord directs his steps. (Proverbs 16:9 NKJ)

Did they have questions in their minds as they followed Jesus daily? Did they ever say, "Jesus, why did you choose me?" Did they know that Jesus was interested in developing their character? After all, the disciples didn't fit the mold of holy men. They were full of jealousy, selfishness, anger, bitterness, fear, doubt, deceit and unforgiveness. When the window of adversity opened did they say, "This is too hard"?

Jesus' teaching was too hard for many to understand. He wanted to teach all of his disciples that they must learn to walk in the spirit and not in the flesh.

When His disciples heard this, many of them said, "This is a hard and difficult and strange saying (an offensive and unbearable message). Who can stand to hear it? (Who can be expected to listen to such teaching)?" (John 6:60 AMP)

Many followed Jesus who had learned of his miracles. They saw the signs and wonders that Jesus performed. Some were students that came to learn but didn't necessarily believe in Jesus. Many came out of curiosity and wanted to see these miracles for themselves. They didn't have spiritual eyes to see or spiritual ears to hear what Jesus was saying.

But Jesus, knowing within Himself that His disciples were complaining and protesting and grumbling about it, said to them: Is this a stumbling block and an offense to you? (Does this upset and displease and shock and scandalize you?) What then (will be your reaction) if you should see the Son of Man ascending to (the place) where He was before?

It is the Spirit who gives life (He is the Life-giver); the flesh conveys no benefit whatever (there is no profit in it). The words (truths) that I have been speaking to you are spirit and life. (John 6:61-63 AMP)

As I was searching for a publisher for my first book *"Touch Me"* I kept saying, "Lord this is your book and you know what publisher you want me to have. I spent months talking with some local authors and listening to their stories, however; it seemed that none of them fit the criteria or expense that I could afford. Then one day a publishing company called me back. We had a wonderful conversation and it looked like this might be the one but I still hadn't heard from the Lord. As I sought God I had this dream that night.

I was driving in a little vehicle by myself. However, I couldn't see so I remained on the side of the road. I had small glasses on. I kept saying, "I can't see." The traffic continued to pass by me on this busy highway. As I continued to have a problem seeing suddenly I looked over on the passenger's seat. I saw a huge pair of glasses sitting on top of the seat. I was so excited and immediately placed them on as I yelled "Now I can see!" Immediately, I drove out into the traffic and the dream ended. When I woke up I asked the Lord what that meant. He showed me that as long as I was looking with my human eyes I couldn't see what he wanted me to see. When I put on my spiritual glasses I could see things from God's perspective.

God showed me that it was time to get out into this traffic. I was no longer going to remain on the side of the road. I woke up that morning with peace in my heart and signed up with the publishing company.

One day I was praying about a situation that looked impossible to accomplish. The Holy Spirit spoke this into my heart. "You should always have a vision greater than yourself to keep reaching higher in your faith in me. When you know there is no way possible for you to accomplish the vision, you will see me bring your impossibilities to my possibilities!"

It is your responsiveness to the Holy Spirit that determines your destiny.

Jesus had been given a vision from His Father. In order for the disciples to share in that vision they would have to have complete faith and confidence in Jesus.

But (still) some of you fail to believe and trust and have faith for Jesus knew from the first who did not believe and had no faith and who would betray Him and be false to Him. And He said, "This is why I told you that no one can come to Me unless it is granted him (unless he is enabled to do so) by the Father." (John 6:64-65 AMP)

The disciples that followed Him in the good times of watching Jesus heal and do many signs and wonders failed to stay with Him.

After this, many of His disciples drew back (returned to their old associations) and no longer accompanied Him. (John 6:66 AMP)

When Jesus asked His twelve disciples if they wanted to leave, this was Peter's response:

Lord, "To whom shall we go? You have the words of eternal life. We believe and know that you are the Holy One of God." (John 6:68-69 NIV)

Did you catch that? Peter not only believed in Jesus but he knew He was the Holy One of God.

How did Peter know that? Before Jesus began to show His disciples that He must go to Jerusalem to suffer, be crucified on the cross and be raised from his death, Jesus asked Peter, "Who do you say that I am?"

He said to them, "But who do you (yourselves) say that I am?" Simon Peter replied, "You are the Christ, the Son of the living God." Then Jesus answered Him, "Blessed (happy, fortunate, and to be envied) are you, Simon Bar-Jonah, for flesh and blood [men] have not revealed this to you, but My Father Who is in heaven." (Matthew 16:15-17 AMP)

In other words, Peter was given spiritual insight to who Jesus was.

Jesus knew the heart of His disciples. He knew who would deny His friendship, betray, doubt His word, follow Him for the miracles, signs and wonders, and love and serve Him with all of their heart.

For many are called (invited and summoned), but few are chosen. (Matthew 22:14 AMP)

Review these questions and ask yourself where you fit in as Jesus disciple. Are you like the ones who followed Him for the miracles, signs and wonders? Or are you following Him because He is the Lord of your life? Have you given the Lord your whole heart?

These people draw near Me with their mouths and honor Me with their lips, but their hearts hold off and are far away from Me. (Matthew 15:8 AMP)

One day during my quiet time the Holy Spirit spoke this into my heart.

"My child when you look at the big picture you can't see my hand in little by little. If I showed you a bigger picture before time you would be overwhelmed. I show you little by little . . . step by step process to reach higher with me. A journey does not take one day. It takes a life time that involves many mistakes along the way. Each one of my children is on a path. Some are stuck at a certain place because they are tired and worn out and need time to rest.

Some of my children look at the end of the climb and get overwhelmed at the time it takes to get there and what it will cost them to achieve it.

Some of my children begin to take a downward spiral because the climb is too hard and too high. They give up and leave the path of righteousness.

The path of adversity becomes too much and they no longer keep the vision ahead of them. Instead they allow all of the negative thoughts to rule and reign in their mind and heart. They begin to take steps backward and the enemy convinces them they will never make it.

Others look at the height. They begin to look down instead of looking up! They allow fear to engulf their hearts and believe satan's words over my WORD!!"

Are you afraid of making mistakes?

Are you tired, worn out and feeling stuck because of the negative thoughts in your mind?

Are you overwhelmed at the time it takes to see answers to your prayers?

Are you looking at what walking the line for Jesus will cost you?

Do you feel you are on a downward spiral since the climb is too hard and too high?

Have you left the path of righteousness and given up on God, yourself and others?

Is the path of adversity too much therefore, you have lost the vision God has given you?

Have you taken some steps backward and allowed the enemy to convince you that you will never make it?

The following is a breathing exercise that the Holy Spirit led me into during one of my quiet times. May I encourage you to speak these words daily!

Breathing exercise

Breathe in his presence for today and let go of your past and future.
Breathe in His faith and let go of all of your fears.
Breathe in His acceptance of you and let out the rejection in your life.
Breathe in His joy that is your strength for today and let go of sorrow.
Breathe in His control over your life and let go of your control.

You will experience His love in ways you have not known. Look inside your heart. Do you see and feel the love that He as for you? God is taking those broken pieces and making a beautiful tapestry. Everything that you have been feeling inside He is bringing to the surface.

God sees your pain and He is calling you to pursue Him.

The definition of pursue is to follow persistently, chase. To advance along the course of, keep to the direction or provisions of a path, plan or system. (Funk and Wagnall)

But as for you, O man of God, flee from all these things; aim at and pursue righteousness (right standing with God and true goodness), godliness (which is the loving fear of God and being Christ like), faith, love, steadfastness (patience), and gentleness of heart. (I Timothy 6:11 AMP)

So Jesus said to those Jews who had believed in Him, "If you abide in My word (hold fast to My teachings and live in accordance with them), you are truly My disciples. And you will know the Truth, and the Truth will set you free." (John 8:31-32 AMP)

And He said to all, "If any person wills to come after Me, let him deny himself (disown himself, forget, lose sight of himself and his own interests, refuse and give up himself) and take up his cross daily and follow Me (cleave steadfastly to Me, conform wholly to My example in living and, if need be, in dying also)." (Luke 9:23 AMP)

Perhaps God has been calling you to come up higher with Him. Maybe the Holy Spirit has been speaking to you about an assignment. I always say, "Lord, I don't want to walk ahead of you or behind you. Help me to walk beside you." Sometimes we receive a prophetic word through others. Instead of waiting on God we try to make it happen. I'd like to encourage you to continually seek God for His timing and His confirmation. If this is from the Lord He will open the doors of opportunity in His timing!

The Holy Spirit began to speak to me over twenty years ago about the calling on my life. However, God knew the preparation that I needed and would have to endure. One night during a very difficult time in my life I had this dream.

The dream started out with my holding a baseball bat in my hand ready to hit the ball. As I waited for the ball to come at me, suddenly I was supernaturally taken from the ball field and placed into an ocean. I began to scream out "Help me. I can't swim!" I felt a hand and found myself being able to float. However, there was so much debris and seaweed that I found myself getting tangled. I tried with all of my might to break out of the entanglement but I couldn't seem to free myself. Again . . . I cried out for help. Suddenly I was out on dry land but as I looked in front of me there were all sizes of rocks. I couldn't go anywhere until I climbed these rocks. Some were so large that I knew there was no way I could climb them.

It was a beautiful sunny day so I decided to get started before the sun went down. I began to climb the smaller ones that led to much larger rocks. As I continued on the smaller rocks the larger rocks were piled up so high that I couldn't see anything behind it. As I climbed these rocks I felt pain all through my body and felt my strength beginning to wane. I had a lot of mixed emotions. Sometimes I felt like I was really conquering this task and other times I felt discouraged and sat down and cried. As I finally came to the last one it was so large that I knew there was no way I could climb this. I cried out for help! Suddenly I felt strong hands lifting me off the rock and placing me on the ground. However, I looked up and saw a huge mountain. This time instead of feeling that I couldn't climb I felt this supernatural energy within me. I was ready to conquer the next task. As I began to climb this mountain I felt a hand quickly lifting me to the top! I was so excited and felt a strong presence surrounding me with peace and joy! Wow! I thought I had arrived. The mission was accomplished! However, suddenly I was taken from the top of the mountain and brought low to the ground. I had no idea where I was but in front of me was a building. I decided to walk in and see if I could find anyone to show me the way. There was a woman who had a towel, washcloth and soap in her hand. She took one look at me and told me to take a shower. Believe me I welcomed this shower since I had been dirty from all of my past adversities. After I was finished showering I eagerly looked forward to talking with the lady since finally I would know where I was. To my dismay she was no longer there. In fact, no one was in the building as I looked all around. I decided to walk outside and suddenly a dense fog moved in. I tried to find my way out of it but to no avail. I was totally engrossed in the smog. I couldn't see my way clear even though I kept looking for a light in this darkness. Finally, I was tired of trying and gave up my will. I had come to the end of my emotions and I could not see the light at the end of this journey. Suddenly I was no longer in the fog but back where I had started. However, this time I was up to bat and Jesus was the pitcher!

And how blessed all those in whom you live, whose lives become roads you travel. They wind through lonesome valleys, come upon brooks, discover cool springs and pools brimming with rain! God-traveled, these roads curve up the mountain, and at the last turn—Zion! God in full view! (Psalm 84:5-7 Message)

Through all of this adversity in my life, I am learning to trust in God who loves me and will never leave or forsake me no matter what adversities or sorrow I may have to go through. Therefore, I can sing of His mercies and know that His loving kindness will follow me all the days of my journey in this life.

Cause me to hear your loving-kindness in the morning, for on You do I lean and in You do I trust. Cause me to know the way wherein I should walk, for I lift up my inner self to you. (Psalm 143:8 AMP)

But I will sing of Your mighty strength and power; yes, I will sing aloud of Your mercy and loving-kindness in the morning; for You have been to me a defense (a fortress and a high tower) and a refuge in the day of my distress. (Psalm 59:16 AMP)

For the love of Christ controls and urges and impels us, because we are of the opinion and conviction that (if) One died for all, then all died; And He died for all, so that all those who live might live no longer to and for themselves, but to and for Him Who died and was raised again for their sake. (II Corinthians 5:14-15 AMP)

Refer to pages 156-159 in the book *"Touch Me"*.

Let's take a glimpse at the new woman and observe the changes that have taken place in her compared to her past life in the New chapter.

- • Has a relationship with the Lord vs. only knowing about Him.

- Knows that she is complete in the Lord vs. focuses on her imperfections.

- Allows the Lord to examine her heart vs. self examination.

- Permits God's acceptance vs. Has a root of rejection.

- Has victory over her past vs. is victim of the past.

- Receives a crown of beauty for the ashes of pain vs. clutches the pain.

- Realizes what Jesus did on the cross for her to be in right standing with Him vs. feeling not good enough, smart enough or pretty enough.

- Focuses on God vs. focuses on herself.

- Overcomes her weaknesses through the power of God vs. helplessness.

- Makes the choice to forgive vs. unforgiveness.

- Believes God's Word which produces faith vs. believing satan's words which produces fear.

- Has the joy of the Lord as her strength vs. hopelessness.

- Attends church with a great expectation for God's word of encouragement for her vs. discouragement.

- Gives encouragement to others vs. not reaching out because of her wounding.

- Displays the fruit of the Spirit vs. no evidence of the Spirit.

- Develops a new nature through the blood of Jesus vs. a sinful nature.

- Puts on the armor of God daily that fights the enemy of her soul vs. fighting in the flesh against people.

- Prepares to meet her groom vs. no preparation

And Jesus replied to him, "It is written, Man shall not live and be sustained on bread alone but by every word and expression of God!" (Luke 4:4 AMP)

Think of this. Every word and expression of God keeps your existence . . . maintains your supply of nourishment, provides fresh manna daily . . . keeps you from falling or sinking in times of trials and tribulations . . . supports your spirit and gives you the vitality needed. It encourages you to keep on keeping on . . . helps you to bear up under difficult circumstances and enables you to experience suffering in the midst of adversity that produces growth in you. It affirms the validity of God's love for you . . . confirms that God's promises are yes and amen. God's word shows us the authority of God is more than sufficiently qualified, adequate for the purpose and capable of changing the impossibilities in your life to His possibilities. Therefore, everything fits together because it properly belongs to God for His perfect plan for your life!

As you have studied this healing guide what changes have taken place in you? What has impacted you the most?

God is coming back for a bride without spot or wrinkle. Are you preparing to meet your groom?

That He might present the church to Himself in glorious splendor, without spot or wrinkle or any such things (that she might be holy and faultless). (Ephesians 5:27 AMP)

Imagine yourself as a bride walking down the aisle ready to be united with your groom. You have spent months and even years preparing for this wondrous event. The day is finally here! There is much hustle and excitement is in the air. Emotions are running high between laughing and crying. You begin to take the first step in coming closer to the man of your dreams. You can't imagine life without him. You have pictured this moment in your mind ever since you were a little girl. Your heart is full of love and totally opened to be his bride.

As you walk closer to your beloved his gaze does not leave you. His eyes are completely on you even though there are many other people around you. He is enthralled by your beauty and can't wait to be joined with you as your husband.

But . . . wait a minute! What would happen if we change the scenario?

What if the bride is late for her own wedding? The wedding march is playing over and over but no bride. Suddenly, she comes in a rush carrying all of her baggage. She didn't have time to lay it down since she has had too much to prepare. She has a huge bag in one arm dragging it behind her since it's too heavy to carry. She has another bag wrapped around her wrist that holds all of her makeup. She couldn't leave that behind. What if she needs a touch up on her face? After all, she really didn't have time to apply all of it properly so it may not last. She carries a bouquet in one hand since she knows that it is an important part of her wedding. She knew that her slip was too big, but she didn't take the time to get another one or have it altered. She thinks to herself, "It will just have to do." Now she has a problem, her slip is beginning to fall closer to her knees. She is wearing a long gown so no one will probably see it; however, it's beginning to get very uncomfortable with each step taken.

He has been waiting many years for her to say I do. When he asked for her hand in marriage, she would always have excuses to keep him waiting. You see, she had so much planned for herself that everyone and everything had to fit into her plans. However, her lover never gave up. He always walked with her in complacency or lack of interest in him.

When she confided in him because of a death of a loved one or suffering in some other way, he was there to listen without judgment or criticism. He placed his arms around her to bring comfort and she would feel safe in his arms.

But there were times when she came through those trials; she made a promise to have a closer relationship with him. But aren't promises made to be broken? After all, she really didn't need him right now. She knew that he would be there to pick her up if she fell. He promised to never leave or forsake her. She knew that his promises are true and his word never returns void. Didn't he promise he would give her the desires of her heart? She knew that he would walk through valleys with her and supply all of her needs. You see, she had just enough knowledge to know about him. She knew all of the characteristics of him. However, she didn't know that she was to allow him to examine her heart. Most of all she didn't realize how much he loved her!

But . . . today is different! This is the day that her groom has been waiting for. Oh! He hasn't tried to change her but has loved her just as she is. He knows that when she becomes his bride, all of the flaws will begin to dissipate. Because of his beckoning call through knocking on the door of her heart for many years, she now opens her heart to receive his love, grace and mercy!

Is your heart open to receive God's love?

When you come to the last chapter in your life what legacy will you leave?

Read pages 160-161 and answer these questions in the book *"Touch Me"*.

Then I heard what sounded like a great multitude, like the roar of rushing waters and like loud peals of thunder, shouting: "Hallelujah! For our Lord God Almighty reigns. Let us rejoice and be glad and give him glory for the wedding of the Lamb has come, and his bride has made herself ready. Fine linen, bright and clean, was given her to wear." (Fine linen stands for the righteous acts of God's holy people.) Then the angel said to me, "Write this: Blessed are those who are invited to the wedding supper of the Lamb!" And he added, "These are the true words of God." (Revelations 19:6-9 NIV)

He has invited you to join Him. Will you come?

Answer Sheet

Touch Me

1. God wants to change us.

2. When we accept Jesus into our heart we receive the gifts of teaching and revelations of the Holy Spirit. We have the mind which contains the counsels and purposes of God that guide, instruct and give knowledge. We hold the feelings and purposes of God's heart.

3. God sees the whole journey of our life from the beginning to the end.

4. Satan's goal is to crush our spirit and harden our heart. God's purpose is to soften our heart and bring life into the deadness of our spirit.

5. To prove what the good, acceptable and perfect will of God is. God's word softens our heart. More darkness is removed and more walls come down.

6. A battle of flesh and spirit begin.

7. When we doubt God's love for us.

8. When a volcano erupts it cannot be stopped. When we receive the power of the Holy Spirit it cannot be contained and flows out to others.

9. **A BOLD UNDEFEATED NEW DARING ABNORMAL NONRESISTANT TAPESTRY!**

Bold

1. With great expectation.

2. Go tell others.

3. God has His perfect timing.

4. She is filled with negative thoughts in her mind.

5. Would God answer her prayer through Jesus?

   Was it her time to be healed?

   Would Jesus come to her?

   Should she touch Jesus?

   Would she have the courage to touch Him or would she cower in fear?

   What if she didn't get healed?

   Would she feel less important?

   Would she dare to risk being rejected?

   Would she be arrested for touching a Jewish man since she was unclean?

   Had she heard anyone say they touched Jesus?

6. She has to throw off all of the negative thoughts and focus on Jesus . . . not the fear.

7. Daughter, your faith (your confidence and trust in me) has made you well.

8.   Apple of God's eye.

9.   Did he feel resentment towards the woman for delaying Jesus?

      Was he angry at Jesus for stopping?

      What kind of a man is this Jesus who heals others and lets a little child die?

Undefeated

1.   Stand up!

      I have given you everything you need.

      My power is within you to conquer the lies of the enemy.

      Look to me my daughter with your head held high.

      You are a child of the King.

      You are royalty.

      Nothing you desire is hidden from you.

      I have given you my favor, anointing and blessing.

      See yourself strong, bold and courageous for that is how I see you.

      See yourself with love pouring out of you for others.

      That love is in you.

      I am inside of you.

      I am love.

Draw from my well of love.

2.   God's love and others.

3.   To show me more of Him and less of me.

4.   Their focus was on the giant (man's undefeated champion) instead of God who is the undefeated Champion of man.

5.   A steep ravine that extended up the middle of the valley.

6.   None. Fear was their greatest enemy.

7.   Fear is listening to satan's words. Faith is listening to God's WORD!

8.   Put away the foreign gods that are among you.

           Incline your heart to the Lord God of Israel.

9.   A man after God's heart.

10.   A man after His heart who would do His will and carry out God's plan.

11.   He heard the spirit of God and the authority God had given to David through his words.

New

1.   She sees herself as not pretty, smart or good enough.

2.   On herself.

3.   She has weaknesses but isn't aware that she needs to give these to God.

4.   She sees herself as a reject and projects that onto others that they will reject her too.

5.   Give her weaknesses to God.

6.   Feels that she has the right to stay angry since it wasn't her fault.

7.   Doesn't realize that perfect love casts out fear.

8.   Doesn't realize that she needs an intimate personal relationship with God.

9.   Feels that God has forgotten her.

10.   She has hidden pain in the closet of her heart that has covered up the gifts.

11.   God's perfect love cast out the fear in my heart and brought an overwhelming love for my dad.

12.   Granting pardon for or remission of something to cease to blame or feel resentment against.

13.   Produces a root of bitterness.

14.   Pain remains hidden.

15.   Readily and freely.

16.   What the person said or did is okay.

17.   Allows God to break satan's destructive hold.

Frees God to restore us emotionally and spiritually.

Allows God's hand to work in our life.

Removes dead weight and gives us back our life.

18. The offense and justification of the anger and gives up the right to hurt the other person back.

19. An apology from the other person.

20. All the time.

21. Choose to forgive immediately and thank God that He has created a clean heart in both of you.

Daring

1. Doubt, unbelief and self pity.

2. Praise God and speak His word over the situations.

3. Selfishness, turmoil, resentment, indifference, fear and ego.

4. Enables our spirit to rise up and become strong to fight the enemy of our soul.

   Directs us on His path and not our own.

   We can still rejoice in God when situations remain unchanged.

Abnormal

1. Zachariah had doubt in his heart that was expressed by asking for a sign which showed lack of faith. He ignored the word from God that came through Gabriel, God's angelic messenger.

   Mary had no doubt and simply trusted God's word through Gabriel.

2. To cast away, worthless, discard, to refuse to accept or recognize. (Funk and Wagnall)

Nonresistant

1. First lesson: Learning the value of relationship with Jesus and what it means to sacrifice and be a committed and devoted servant to Him.

   Second lesson: Jesus separated the sin of this woman and saw her brokenness and repentant heart. It's easier to see the outward sin of others but a lot harder to see the sin in our own heart.

2. Give God your mind and acknowledge the sin of these negative thoughts.

   Begin a word process (speak God's word over the negative thoughts).

   Nip it in the bud and do not entertain those thoughts.

3. The mind is a play ground for the devil.

   Be honest with your thoughts to God.

   Don't allow the enemy to wreak havoc in your mind.

   When the enemy comes in like a flood, take God's sword and rise up against him.

   When you speak God's word you will have victory in your mind.

4. We lack firmness of purpose in our life.

5. When we allow satan into our thoughts.

6.   Kill, steal and destroy.

7.   For us to have an abundant life.

8.   Loving God with all our minds.

9.   Satan.

10.   Speaking God's word over ourselves.

11.   Our soul is refreshed and God has the victory over the enemy.

Tapestry

None

About the Author

Jenny Hagemeyer was born in Altoona, PA and at the age of six, ran to the altar out of a fear of going to hell and accepted the Lord into her heart at a Christian & Missionary Alliance Church. Her parents later moved to Lancaster County, PA where she grew up and graduated from high school. Her desire was to be a missionary and attend a Bible school but unforeseen circumstances took place and didn't allow that to happen. She met a young man after graduation and married him at the age of eighteen years old. Throughout those years Jenny taught Sunday school, held Bible studies in her home, good news club for children and counseled at church camps. However, in those years, she only knew God as a Bible God.

In 1982 Jenny received the Baptism of the Holy Spirit in an Aglow meeting that her friend had taken her too. As an adult she would still cower in fear while praying and telling God that she was a bad girl. One day as she was praying she heard the Holy Spirit say, "What kind of a God do you think I am?" In 1983 a bombshell was dropped on her that would change the rest of her life. Her son was diagnosed with severe scoliosis, her husband of fifteen years left on her daughter's twelfth birthday, their dog was put to sleep and her uncle died suddenly whom she loved. This began her journey to a more intimate relationship with the Lord. One night, during the separation, the Lord spoke to her in an audible voice. He told her that He was going to use her to heal his people. He said, "You must be able to hear my voice!" Jenny had no idea how God could use her while she was so distraught in her emotions that there was no way she could help herself let alone other people!

In 1987 Jenny married Fred from Mifflin County, PA whom she met in a Christian singles group in Lancaster County. After Jenny remarried she felt a strong calling from God to be used in ministry and began to seek the Lord for His direction and guidance.

In 1998 she started a women's weight loss group in her home. The Lord gave her a vision of a heart that looked like a puzzle with many pieces. Beside the heart was a bag of presents. God showed Jenny that when she gave those pieces, such as anger, unforgiveness, selfishness, pride, fear, jealousies and so forth over to Him the blessings would come such as peace, love, joy, patience, goodness, meekness, kindness, gentleness and self control. God showed Jenny that her heart was clogged like a drain gets clogged in a sink and she needed His Drano of love to penetrate those darkened areas in her heart. The women's group consisted of women of different denominations and backgrounds. As Jenny and the other women talked with one another, they realized they all had low self esteem and didn't like themselves! As God began to reveal those areas in Jenny, she began to teach those lessons weekly to the other women. God began a healing process in Jenny's past that has enabled her to teach it out to others. As she yielded to the Holy Spirit He placed a message in her heart. He told her, "It's time to heal the church to heal the world!"

As Jenny and the other women began to pray Psalm 26:2 daily that says, "Test me, O Lord and try me, examine my heart and my mind for your love is ever before me and I walk continually in your truth," God began to reveal areas in their heart that needed healed. They learned to lay them at Jesus feet and ask him to change them! As they opened the door to the closet of their heart that contained fear, unforgiveness, selfishness and pride, and so forth God began construction in all of them.

In 2001 the Holy Spirit spoke into her heart, "Thank me that you are teaching the Battle Plan to the Promised Land." Two months later she was impressed of the Holy Spirit to begin writing. She had no idea on how to write the Battle Plan. God reminded her of a flower bank in her back yard that had been overgrown by weeds. When she focused on the weeds, she felt overwhelmed and didn't know where to begin. The Holy Spirit had spoken into her heart, "Take a section at a time." He showed her that is exactly what He was going to do in writing the Battle plan . . . one section at a time. One year later Jenny had her first women's renewal in a Methodist Church in Clarion County, PA.

Fred and Jenny, married 24 years, reside in Belleville, PA and have <u>Promise Land Ministries</u> that consists of a <u>team</u> that was formed to bring health, healing and wholeness to everyone in all walks of life. She is a wife, mother and grandmother of eleven grandchildren. Jenny teaches how God brought her into a personal relationship with Him and shares her journey through pain and suffering. She has mentored and prayed with many women and still continues while taking the ministry out to other counties and states.

Jenny is the author of the book *"Touch Me"* written under the inspiration of the Holy Spirit that shares her journey to a more intimate relationship with the Lord that brought healing to her heart and mind. It is a life giving book that brings encouragement in which Jenny shares openly the locked emotions that became imprisoned in her heart, negative thoughts that she entertained and hurtful words that were spoken about her and to her. She shares her testimony of how God led her to put the WORD into action in not only being a hearer of the word but a doer! Ultimately, God led her into a teaching of what God's desire of an abundant life represents. She is a speaker called by God to take His message of love out to the highways and byways. Jenny is licensed to minister with Global Ministries through the Worship Center in Lancaster County, PA. The ministry is available for retreats, renewals, workshops, special programs and other events. Every ministry event is tailored by the Holy Spirit to meet the emotional, physical, and spiritual needs of the people. For more information on Promise Land Ministries see the blog at promiselandministries.wordpress.com

To contact Jenny e-mail fred87jen@embarqmail.com

Please include a testimony of how this book has touched your heart.

Also By Jenny Hagemeyer

Touch Me

(Companion book to "Touch Me Guide to Healing")

Available at:

Local Bookstores
Amazon.com
Barnes and Noble
iUniverse.com
Books A Million

References

Funk and Wagnall Dictionary. New York: Harper and Row Publishers, 1984

Nelson Study Bible, NKJ. Nashville: Thomas Nelson Publishers, 1982

Strong, James. The New Strong's Exhaustive Concordance of the Bible. Nashville: Thomas Nelson Publishers, 1984